Edwin Exon

Lyrical Drama, Poems, and Translations

Edwin Exon

Lyrical Drama, Poems, and Translations

ISBN/EAN: 9783744780025

Printed in Europe, USA, Canada, Australia, Japan

Cover: Foto ©Thomas Meinert / pixelio.de

More available books at **www.hansebooks.com**

PRESS NOTICES.

THE AUSTRALASIAN (*Melbourne*).

The story (Apotheosis of Hercules) comprehends the death and translation of Hercules. The work is divided into three parts, named respectively Olympus, Euboea, and Mount Æta. It is deserving of careful analysis, and might profitably and deservedly be taken, passage by passage, in measuring the extent to which it interprets the sense of the fable.

MELBOURNE AGE.

Mr. Exon's literary capacity was only lately referred to complimentarily . . . and he has now again the opportunity of showing, not only literary capacity, but a true poetic instinct that has enabled him to furnish Mr. Plumpton with a powerfully dramatic poem ("Endymion"), very compact as a work, and pure both in style and expression. The "Argument" . . . gives but a dim idea of the beauty which characterises its poetic development.

MELBOURNE HERALD.

The "Victorian Jubilee Ode," . . . whose pleasing and patriotic lines and inspiriting and graceful setting recalled to mind the line:

"Perfect music set to noble words."

MONTHLY CIRCULAR (*S. Mullen, Melbourne*).

As a literary composition, the "Victorian Jubilee Ode" is exceptionally good. It breathes with the true spirit of poetic fervour and patriotism, its exalted tone and musical rhythm reminding one of the work of the great Dryden more than of that of any other of our national poets.

Lyrical Dramas

Poems

AND

Translations

BY

EDWIN EXON

MELBOURNE
SAMUEL MULLEN, COLLINS STREET EAST
LONDON: 29, LUDGATE HILL
1888

	PAGE
LYRICAL DRAMAS—	
Endymion	9
The Apotheosis of Hercules	28
MISCELLANEOUS POEMS—	
Savonarola. Frà Angelico...	39
Lago Maggiore	43
The Music of Nature	45
In Memoriam	48
The Angel's Prayer	49
The Victorian Jubilee Ode	51
The Higher Life	58
The Dream of Olaf	60
TRANSLATIONS—	
Iphigenia in Tauris. Goethe. (Acts first and last, with a connecting account of the Story of the Drama) ...	65
The God and the Bayadere. Goethe	116
Wanderlied. Kuntz	123
Waldabendschein	125
SUGGESTIONS, EXTRACTS, &c.—	
Rutli Meadow, and the Swiss Confederacy ...	129
The Universe	130
The Conservation of Energy	130
Buddhism	130
Agnosticism	132
The Unknowable	133
Utilitarianism and Materialism	134
Materialism in Religion	134
The Power of Thought	135
The Doctrine of Necessity	136
The Great Centre	137
The Falls at Tivoli	139
Notes to Savonarola	141

LYRICAL DRAMAS.

ENDYMION:
A LYRICAL DRAMA.

Performed by the Metropolitan Liedertafel Society of Melbourne.

Music by ALFRED PLUMPTON.

The incidents of the story are Selected and Arranged from the Poem by Keats.

ARGUMENT.

PROLOGUE.

ENDYMION, fatigued with hunting, rests in a grove. The Goddess Diana finds him sleeping there; loves him, and inspires him in his sleep with a consuming but mysterious and dreamlike passion for her.

The Fates declare union between them impossible until Endymion is freed from mortality.

PART I.

Festival of the God Pan, presided over by Endymion and his sister Peona. First come children with garlands waiting for the festival. Soft music swells and dies away. Damsels approach, singing and dancing. Shepherds join them. Hunters follow. Endymion, distraught with passion, wanders away from the festival into the forest followed by his sister, while the aged priest leads the hymn of praise to Pan.

Part II.

Endymion leaves his sister, and near a fountain is met by a Nereid, who tells him he must journey far, even beyond the bounds of mortality, before he can lose his anguish in the bosom of an Immortal Love. She directs him to a cavern in the depths of the earth.

In the ocean caverns Endymion rescues Glaucus from the enchantments of Circe, and restores to life a multitude of dead lovers. They all assemble in Neptune's palace, and are joined by Aphrodite and Eros. Amid the glorious revelry before the Water Monarch, the mortal senses of Endymion are overpowered and he sinks in a swoon at the feet of Neptune, with a prayer to Diana. The Nereids bear him up to earth, Diana revealing herself to his inner senses, and promising him speedy bliss.

Epilogue.

Diana, disguised as a dark-eyed Indian Beauty, a Votaress of Pleasure and a reveller with Bacchus, tempts Endymion. He feels strangely drawn to her and partly yields, though all the while conscious of a higher and purer love. In despair of realizing it, torn by conflicting passions and professing his unworthiness, he consecrates himself to a hermit's life, takes farewell of the Indian Beauty and his sister, who dedicate themselves to the vestal service of Diana. He appoints a last meeting with them. His last request (to know Heaven's will on their sad fate) is granted by the Indian lady, who, resuming her true form as the Goddess Diana, translates Endymion, spiritualized and free from mortality, to eternal union with herself in the heavens.

PROLOGUE.

SCENE. *A glade in a forest by moonlight. Diana bending in rapt admiration over the sleeping Endymion.*

Diana—
  O wondrous dream of loveliness!
   A star hath fallen from the skies!
  Apollo's peer, in mortal dress
   Lies slumbering here before mine eyes.

  O Jove, this perfect work of thine,
   This wonder of delight,
  Earth's crowning gem to me, divine,
   In holy love unite.

 Come, gentle darkness; softly hide the bliss
 Of souls uniting in a virgin kiss.
 (*She stoops to kiss Endymion. Enter the Fates.*)

Diana—
 Wherefore, dire messengers, come ye?

The Fates—
    Bend, and receive the Fates' decree :
    When thou from mortal bonds canst set him free
    Then only may Endymion wed with thee.
        (*The Fates disappear.*)

Diana (*bending over Endymion and again kissing him*)—
    Celestial sleep seal fast thine eyes,
        Sweet dreams of Heav'n enthrall thy soul,
    Thy spirit, linked with mine, shall rise
        To spheres where suns unnumbered roll
    Their shining orbs, a glorious zone
    Encircling the All Father's throne.

    Then, when awaked, to earth returning,
        Dim memories, like a pleasing pain
    Shall fill thee with mysterious yearning,
        And never shalt thou rest again
    Until the way is found for thee
    To rise from earth, and mate in heaven with me.

        END OF PROLOGUE.

PART I.

Scene I. *Forest on Mount Latmos at early dawn. An altar on a wide lawn prepared for the Festival of Pan.*

(*Enter children with flowers and garlands.*)

(*Song of the children waiting for the beginning of the festival.*)

The long, long hours of night have passed,
The prayed-for morning comes at last,
While others slept, our fingers weaved
These altar garlands, ivy leaved,
And floral crowns, whose lovely hues
Are freshened with still falling dews.

(*They pause and look around. Soft music is heard.*)

Silent and desert still the sacred spot!
O tardy worshippers, why come ye not?

Hush! a sweet sound is floating by!
Is it of earth, or air, or sky?
It swells, fades, dies, revives again.
Great Pan—Whence comes that Heavenly strain?

(The soft music is repeated, gradually swelling to a loud and joyful strain leading into a dance measure, as damsels and shepherds come singing and dancing.)

Damsels—
      From your rivers, lakes, and mountains,
         Nymphs, whose love-inspiring glow
      Flushes the immortal fountains
         Whence the loves of mortals flow,
      Play about us in the dancing
         Leaves upon the breezy hills;
      Laugh upon us in the glancing
         Sunbeams; murmur in the rills,
      Till ye fill our hearts to madness
      With the anguish of Love's gladness.

Then hie ye, unseen, to each meadow and grove
Where lost in fond day-dreams our young shepherds rove.
Songs, full of tenderest passion, O sing them—
Heart full of love, to our feet O bring them.

Shepherds—
      Ere yet the morning's tender rays
         Burn into noonday heat,
      We come through sweet, wild, woodland ways
         Our loving fair to meet.
They come!—the play of sunlit waves—the light of summer skies
Are in their merry dances, and their love-illumined eyes.

Damsels and Shepherds—
    Joy is everywhere,
        The Spirit of Love is abroad,
    And the music in the air
        Is breathed by the lips of a God.

(*The notes of a hunting-horn are heard. Hunters enter singing.*)

Hunters' Song—
    The red dawn flames in the Eastern sky,
    As away, to the gallant hunt we hie;
    Endymion—lord of the chase—shall lead
    With the lion's strength and the eagle's speed.
    Hark! through the merry woods ring out
    The hound's deep bay, and the hunter's shout.

    The savage prey, with crouching form
        And gleaming tusks, deep hidden lies.
    Pan startles him with a sudden alarm—
        Away through the forest in terror he flies.
        At bay, he glares with despairing eyes.
    The hounds are upon him, his race is o'er;
        He is under the ban
        Of the great god Pan,
    And our flocks shall dread his fangs no more.
        The day is done,
        The prey is won,
    In triumph let Pan and his wood-nymphs hear
    The horn, and the clash of the hunting spear;

And the darkling woods ring merrily out
With the hound's deep bay and the hunter shout.

(Enter Endymion and his sister Peona, with the aged priest of Pan, bearing offerings. During the singing of the following hymn, Endymion, with a pale and distracted countenance, gazes restlessly about him, and, after a brief space, wanders into the forest, followed by his sister.)

The Priest—
Now to the altar. Hunters, shepherd swains,
And you, ye gentle maids and children, come;
No heart must fail to-day, no tongue be dumb.
Rich bounty Pan hath poured, praise him in loftiest strains.

(They all gather near. The children form an inner circle round the altar, and lay their garlands upon it. Endymion and Peona stand at the right hand of the priest, who pours the offering as the people sing their hymn of praise to Pan.)

The ripened grain like seas of gold,
Are rolling o'er each fertile field,

And multiplied a thousand fold
   Our teeming flocks and orchards yield.
O bounteous Pan ! the source of all
   Art thou ! To thee our thanks we bring.
Hear us, as on thy gracious name we call—
   Hear us, O Shepherd King.

Come not in terrors clad to-day ;
   Shake not the mountains in thy wrath ;
With Echo, through the forests play,
   Bid Naiads dance about thy path,
With love-songs fill the murmuring woods,
   Spread flowers where'er thy feet have trod
By silver streams in sylvan solitudes—
   Hear us, O Forest God.

The grandeur of the towering hills,
   The charms of peaceful vales are thine ;
Thine is the quickening breath that fills
   The earth clod with a soul divine.
The mystic spell of prophet lore,
   The poet's power, with thee began ;
All praise be thine with worship evermore—
   Hear us, O mighty Pan.

SCENE II. *A distant part of the forest whither Endymion has wandered from the festival, followed by his sister Peona.*

Peona—
   Alas, my brother! From the sacred place
     And from the people's joy, why thus withdrawn?
   As is the sun in heaven, so is thy face
     To them. With thee, their light is gone.

Endymion—
   Dark clouds are o'er me. Tears hide all
     The world, save where one far-off gleam
   Of vague wild hope uplifts the pall.
     I live but in the memory of a dream.

Was it a dream? My queen! My queen!
   No mortal could have shaped in thought
The beauty that mine eyes have seen;
   O let my soul again be caught
Away from earth in blissful rest,
Upborne to heaven on thy sweet breast.

THE DREAM.

   I saw the earth sink down. Red Mars
     And Venus on our faces glowed;
   We soared until th' approaching stars
     Grew into suns. The dread abode

Lyrical Dramas.

Of the Celestial Powers drew near,
Joy changed to awe, and love to fear.

Closer I felt thy loving arms,
 The dreadful splendours of the skies
Chastened their light in thy sweet charms,
 Looked love upon me from thine eyes,
And drew my soul beyond the line
That severs mortal from divine.

Now, thirsting for a joy above
 All joys that earth can ever give,
I wander, seeking thee, my love,
 For thee content to die or live.
I have no being of mine own,
Thine am I; thine, and thine alone!

END OF PART I.

PART II.

SCENE I. *A secluded part of the forest, Endymion wandering alone near a fountain.*

Endymion—
    As lofty as have been my dreams of thee,
    Sweet Queen in Heaven, so deep my fall must be
    Distracted, hopeless, wand'ring, cast away!
    Some gentle guidance grant me, gods, I pray.

A Nereid (speaking unseen from the fountain)—
    Kneel at the fountain by thy side,
    There bathe thine eyes and see thy guide.

    (*As he kneels the Nereid appears.*)
    In all thy wanderings I have been
    Thy Heaven-sent guide, unknown, unseen.
      Turn now to yonder cave,
    Plunge boldly o'er the dizzy steep,

For thou must reach a lower deep
   Than ocean's deepest grave.
Dark way to glorious end is thine
Thou chosen love of one divine.

    (*Endymion enters the cavern.*)

SCENE II. *A vast hollow under the bed of the sea, the murmur of ocean heard far above. Upon the floor of the vault, innumerable dead bodies. At the entrance sits a man with a wand of pearl in his hand reading a scroll open on his knee, his feet entangled in a mat of frozen weed, his face deeply-furrowed with age and misery. Endymion approaches him.*

Endymion—
    O sorrow-laden figure, what art thou?

Glaucus—
    Once Glaucus, till myself I rendered up
To Circe's foul enchantment; therefore now
   The bitter dregs of her accursed cup
I drain, in penance bound a thousand years
To living death in chains of frozen tears.

Endymion—
    And what are these?
            (*Pointing to the dead bodies.*)

Glaucus— Dead lovers they,
 Awaiting one who from the face of day
 Will turn, for their deliverance, and mine.

Endymion—
 O would that I were he!

Glaucus— A light divine
 Is breaking from thee as thou speakest,
 Tell me what, in this prison house, thou seekest.

Endymion —
 The ardour of new kindling fire,
  As from the gods, within me burns.
 Jove, thou hast changed my deep desire,
  Dreams—sick desires—my spirit spurns.
 Power for a god-like deed I crave,
 Be this, of every hope, the crown or grave.

Glaucus—
 Awake! rejoice! the hour, the man is come!

(*Endymion takes the pearl wand and strikes with it on the pillar of the chamber. A wonderful sound is evoked, multiplied by the echoes, and woven into exquisite harmonies. The roof opens, and the multitudes pour into the palace hall of Neptune.*)

Endymion—
>The ocean trembles as the storm-like roll
>>Of harmony, in waves of awful sound,
>>Too dread for mortal hearing, spread around.
>My heart and brain are bursting; yea, my soul
>Sinks, overwhelmed! Diana! Help! I die!

Neptune—
>Quick, Nereids, to his rescue fly!
>His o'erwrought soul in slumber steep,
>Then bear him earthward from the deep.

(*Endymion is borne to earth. Diana speaks to him in a vision.*)

Diana—
>Dearest, my heart is sore for thee
>And yet no other way could be.
>Only through seas of deepest pain
>Thy heaven, so lofty, could'st thou gain.
>Keep steadfast heart through one sharp trial more,
>Then be with me in bliss for evermore.

END OF PART II.

EPILOGUE.

SCENE—*Latmos. The home of Endymion. Peona awaiting the arrival of Endymion and the Indian lady, who come from the forest, walking apart, with heads drooping.*

Peona—
>Dear brother, and fair sister, why
>>So sadly come ye? Is not this
>The hour which brings ye from the sky
>>Jove's mandate for your perfect bliss?
>So the diviners read the sign
>To-day beheld on Cynthia's shrine.

Endymion (to the Indian lady)—
>Farewell! and with farewell to thee,
>>Farewell to life! The sacred fire,
>Wherewith the gods had gifted me
>>Lo, I have sunk in low desire.
>A hermit, from the world I fly;
>With life alone my shame can die.

The Indian Lady—
>These eyes that tempted thee shall waste
>   Henceforth in penitential tears.
>To Cynthia's temple service chaste
>   I dedicate my future years.
>Yet once more, O lost love divine,
>Meet me at Dian's sacred shrine.

SCENE LAST. *The grove behind Diana's temple. Beside the altar are seen Peona and the Indian lady closely veiled. A vesper hymn is heard.*

HYMN.

>Night to vexèd earth has given
>   Rest from tumults, sins, and wars.
>In th' unfathomed depths of heaven
>   O'er the silence reign the stars.
>One purple cloud rides high o'er earth and sea,
>There Cynthia's chariot waits.—But where is she?

Peona—
>Here, brother, stay thy weary wandering feet,
>What would'st thou—ere our offering is complete?

Endymion—
>Nought but to know the will of Heaven.

The Indian Lady (unveiling, and revealing herself as Diana)—

                         'Tis done;
And thou thine immortality hast won.
So falls from thee the last of earthly leaven,
And thou art mine for evermore in heaven.

    Long was the trial; deep the pain,
      And dark the troubled past:
    Greater the glory; worthier thou
      To gain the crown at last.
    Now is thy day of triumph come,
      O my belov'd arise
    From the dull earth to share with me
      Love's empire in the skies.

Chorus.

  Diana lifts on high her silver bow,
And as the floods of glory pour around,
  Celestial songs reply to hymns below.
" The link uniting earth to heaven is found—
Endymion with immortal love is crowned."

THE END.

THE APOTHEOSIS OF HERCULES:

A LYRICAL DRAMA.

Written for the Melbourne Liedertafel.

Music by Alfred Plumpton.

ARGUMENT.

The first scene is in Olympus, where the Immortals are rejoicing over the approaching Apotheosis of Hercules, but Jove declares that a deadly trial awaits him, and sends Hermes to warn him.

The second scene is at Eubœa. Hercules, erecting an altar, receives the message from Jove, and Lichas brings him, from Deianira, the white robe in which he is to offer sacrifice. The robe has been anointed with a subtle poison given by Nessus, under the pretence that it is a love charm, to Deianira, who, in a fit of jealousy, has used it for the purpose of securing to herself the love of her husband. Hercules puts on the robe, and the poison fastens upon him, eating with the robe into his flesh.

The last scene is on Mount Oeta. Hercules, in his agony, casts himself into the flames of the altar prepared for sacrifice. As he lies in the fire, Nessus and a chorus of Demons exult in his torment, and in their apparent triumph over the son of Jove. Hercules, for awhile despairing, supplicates his father's aid. Hermes appears, strengthening him. As the flesh of Hercules consumes, the flames die down into a clear radiance, from which his glorified form is seen rising towards heaven.

At the gate of heaven Hercules is met by Hebe, who, amid the acclamations of the Deities, presents him with the garland of Perpetual Youth and the crown of Immortal Love.

SCENE I. *Olympus.*

Chorus of Immortals—
    Over the bright celestial plains and hills
        Where joy and bliss supreme for ever dwell
    A warmer glow of heavenly radiance thrills,
        And louder songs of praise and triumph swell.
    Th' Olympian mountains tremble at the strain :
        The name of Hercules—by every tongue
    From heaven to earth and back to heaven again
        In mighty tempest of acclaim is flung—
            Hercules ! Hercules !

Incarnate strength of God on earth,
   Victor in work and warfare crowned,
Cast off thy mould of mortal birth!
   Henceforth enthroned in heaven be found—
      Hercules! Hercules!

But see! The clouds that veil the seat
   Of Jove, roll back! The Thunderer calls
Hermes, who hastes with wingèd feet,
   And at the father's footstool falls.

Jove (*to Hermes*)—
   Fly earthward, Hemes! My all-conquering son
Too soon believes his final victory won;
Warn him that, by the Fates permitted yet
   To rage in mad rebellion 'gainst the skies,
A deadlier power than he has ever met,
   With subtle snare, unseen before him lies.

      Scene II. *Euboea.*

(*Hercules erecting an altar; he receives from Hermes the warning sent by Jove, and from Lichas the white robe anointed with poison, sent to him by Deianira.*)

Hercules (*to Hermes*)—
   Thanks, Hermes! Tho' thy message bodeth ill,
The word of Jove to me is welcome still.

And if the foe be his, no less than mine,
The triumph must remain with power divine.

Hermes—

The time may come when thou shalt doubt Heav'n's might.

Hercules—

It hath been so in many a hero fight!
In the dark hour of agony supreme
His foes shriek triumph o'er him. As a dream
The tumult passes, like the last wild roar
Of waves at maddest height dash'd on a rocky shore.
    Jove grant that when my foes shall rave
        In the dread final shock,
    They, may be as the shattered wave,
        And I, the unshaken rock.

Hermes—

    Jove wills that when thy foes shall rave
        In the dread final shock,
    They shall be as the scatter'd wave,
        And thou th' unshaken rock.

Hercules—

    But now, to holy thoughts subdued,
        For this white robe I lay aside
    Spoil of fierce war, and weapon rude,
        My club, and rugged lion-hide.

(He clothes himself in the white garment from Deianira the poison fastens on him.)

Hercules—
    Ah, Lichas! Wretch! What hast thou done?
    Art thou the hidden treach'rous one?

(In his agony he hurls Lichas into the sea. Nessus appears.)

Nessus—
    Still he consumes in anguish! Vain
    All struggle! Struck to heart and brain,
    Past help! His very blood is bane,
    And every nerve and sinew—pain!

Hercules—
    Bear me to Oeta, quickly there
    For a burnt sacrifice prepare.

Scene III. *Mount Oeta.*

(The funeral pyre of Hercules.)

Nessus *(and Shades from Tartarus)*—
    Shadows of departed dread
    To the realms of Hades fled,
    Lift your hydra heads again,
    Your great enemy is slain!
    Gather round his funeral pile,
    In his death-throes him revile
    By whose prowess we were hurled
    To the gloomy underworld.

CHORUS.

Gather round his funeral pile!
In his death-throes him revile
By whose prowess we were hurled
To the gloomy underworld.

Come from every darksome den
　Lurking powers of evil might—
Haters all of gods and men—
　Poisoning earth in Jove's despite!
Hydra-headed serpent brood,
　Dragons! Beasts! resume your reign!
Hercules is now subdued
　Rise and ravage earth again!

Gather round his funeral pile,
In his death-throes him revile
By whose prowess we were hurled
To the gloomy underworld.

Hercules (from the fire)—

Father divine! Almighty Lord!
If this dread doom be my reward
Will not thy service be abhorr'd
And thou be never more adored?
Not for myself alone I cry—
Jove's glory fades, if thus I die.

Nessus (*to Hercules*)—
>No answer cometh to thy prayer
>>Save from the tongues of hissing flames.
>What should the heavens know, or care,
>>Of pangs that dwell in mortal frames?
>Thou boaster of celestial birth
>Despair, and die—poor son of earth!

Hermes (*to Hercules*)—
>If strength divine to thee belong,
>In suff'ring, as in fight, be strong!
>Fear not the flames, they will but slay
>All that can suffer or decay,
>Sacred baptismal fires are they
>Purging the taint of earth away.

Chorus of Mortals—
>Art thou, O Jove, the enemy of good?
>>Or do th' infernal powers o'ermatch thine own?
>Behold our greatest! and thy son! subdued!
>>A prey to mocking fiends in torture thrown.

>Now o'er the lurid scene a blinding flash
>>Of lightning hurtles through the riven air,
>And rolling thunder's overwhelming crash
>>At length th' almighty power of Jove declare.
>A tempest sweeps the mocking fiends away;
>>The altar flames become celestial light;

The Apotheosis of Hercules.

Hercules, like a new-born king of day
    Uprising, dazzles the beholder's sight ;
Unearthly music trembles through the air :
    Unearthly glory fills the awestruck eye.
Arrayed in rosy light, the Goddess fair
    Of Youth and Love to Hercules draws nigh,
And the sweet waving of her radiant wings
Celestial odours spreads, as thus she sings :

Hebe (to Hercules)—

    Heav'n opens wide its shining gate !
        Gods rend the skies with songs divine,
    And Jove himself in awful state
        Unveils the glory of his shrine.
    At his right hand behold thy throne,
        In me, his crowning gift approve.
    In me, he gives thee for thine own
        Undying Youth—Eternal Love.

Earth vibrates to the strain, Heav'n's arches ring,
Whilst gods and men unite thy praise to sing,
        Hercules ! Hercules !
Thou wert the strength of God on earth,
    Victor in work and warfare crowned ;
Now, freed from taint of mortal birth,
    For ever throned in Heaven be found —
        Hercules ! Hercules !

MISCELLANEOUS POEMS.

SAVONAROLA—FRÀ ANGELICO.

[Lines written in Florence, April, 1888, after a visit to the Church and Convent of St. Mark's, and the place opposite the Palazzo Vecchio, where Savonarola and his two friends were executed.]

        FLORENCE!—
Well named the Fair! Of all thy loveliness
What shall my memory retain?
        Two names—
Savonarola—Frà Angelico.
Angelico! For thee the monkish cell
Was not a refuge for a timid soul
Anxious for self in this world or the next—
Thy Prayer was Labour, and thy Labour, Prayer—
Thy painter's art, a holy gift. No face
Or figure wouldst thou paint for hire.
Upon thy knees, before the cross, was sought,
And found, the inspiration of thy work.
Then, as the heav'n-born thought or feeling came,
Thy soul, aflame with fervent piety,
Through sleepless nights of prayer and tears would form
Visible images of things unseen,

Ethereal, divine, and spiritual,
Which then, in eager haste, thine hands would fix
Upon the convent walls, or in the cells [1]
Where simple men, uplifting eyes in prayer,
From early dawn to night might plainly read
The passion and the love of Christ the Lord
And of his holy followers.   Thy labour
In sacred passion lasted till the power
Of the divine Afflatus, overpassed,
Forsook thee : then the brush was laid aside
And never after was the holy work
Profaned with colder touch.

Savonarola !   May the memory
Of thee dwell ever in the minds of men
To lift them from the common mire of self
As nearly as their natures may attain
The level of thy holy, hero spirit.
Like unto us wert thou in weaker moments : [2]
God grant that at our best we may become
At least a little like to thee.   Once more
Stand imag'd in my thought.—First as a youth ;
Thy boyish love proudly repell'd with scorn—
And thou as proudly flinging back the scorn.[3]
Then, with a nobler love, that loving, much
Above the common, father—mother—kindred—
Forsook them all for One above them all ;

[1] For Notes, see end of the book, page 141.

Or, rather, sanctified and merged all love
In love of God and all His suffering people.[4]
I see thee, as the toiling pilgrim, come
To Florence, faint and weary unto death—
Thy frame too weak for thy great soul in travail.[5]
Then, as the preacher—treated first with scorn
By polished courtiers, fasting then with tears [6]
Deeming the fault thine own. But fire from heaven
Consumed thee till thy tongue gave forth its message,
And soon the proudest of the princely tyrants
And the unholy pontiff, caring not
For God or man, at last became afraid
Of thee. The people loved thee as their Saviour
And worshipped thee, and served thee till the arts
Of princely and of priestly enemies
Blinded and drove them mad. They rudely tore thee
Buffeted, spit upon, and cursed, to prison—
Tortured thee, till the frenzy of thy pain
Forced from thee falsehoods which thy foes desired
Against thyself, but not the lies they craved
To slay thy friends. They hanged and burned thee, there
Where flows the fountain now at Neptune's foot.[7]
The multitude for whom thy life was given
Thronged round thee in thy dying agony
To make thy last hour bitter with their hate.
Thy burning eloquence had been their shield
Against oppressors: now, no word hadst thou
To shame them for their baseness—one last look

Alone replied to them. Over the raging mass
One dying glance of love and pity lingered
Till the consuming agony of death
Veiled from thee all the sins and woes of earth.

RETURN AT EVENING FROM ISOLA BELLA OVER LAKE MAGGIORE.

HALF-WAY across the lake the evening shadows,
Advancing from the Western mountains, creep
Towards the East.   The brilliant hues of day
Pale into softer beauties.   Morn and Noon
Had purpled o'er the waters—touched with flame
Of pure white glory distant snowy summits
Of mountains blending with the shining clouds—
Covered the hills with violet flushed with rose,
The fields with vivid emerald—the woods
With darker hues of green and glowing bronze.
But now the glory melts to quiet shades
Save where, in pearly grey, the brightness lingers.

Onward the growing shadow slowly sweeps :
It covers all the lake—touches the shore—
Rolls up the Eastern mountains—overflows
The last far distant summit.   Night is come—
Deep, silent, calm, and peaceful !   Not in gloom !
The stars in multitudes are looking down
From the blue vault above, and gleaming up,
Reflected, from the deep blue wave below.

There comes a silent majesty of calm—
An infinite, unutterable peace,
And faithful souls recall with solemn joy
The word divine. "*My peace I give to you.*
"*Not as the world gives, give I unto you.*"

LOVE REIGNETH OVER ALL.

AN ODE TO MUSIC.

Sung by the Metropolitan Liedertafel of Melbourne.

Music by Professor Elsässer.

I.

The Seas, the Lakes, the Mountains, and the Trees
Are living presences; and he who sees
Beneath the surface, till this truth be known,
Is never less alone, than when alone.

II.

Music everywhere
Spreading wide as sunlight and air
Fills the open ear
With a harmony full and clear.
Grand—when the fierce storm is pouring
  Wrath on the forest and mountains;
Sweet—when the birds' songs are soaring
  Over the meadows and fountains;

  Wild—when ocean deep,
With the throb of the storm in its waves,
  Springs with thundering leap
At the rocks and the roaring caves.

III.

But the purest, grandest tones that float around
Earth and heaven, are but empty sound
Till responsive souls receive and raise the tone
Into songs and anthems of their own.

IV.

  Rest, weary heart!
   Gently murmur the rills;
  Hope thou in God!
   Sing the forest-clad hills:
Storm stirs the soul, like a battle song, cheering the fight
  In the conflict for Right.

V.

Thunder's roll and the fierce Lightning's ray
Drive fell vapours and dark mists away,
Clearing the heavens for a brighter day.
  Tempest and darkness receding,
  Splendour of sunshine succeeding,
Beauty clothes the earth in her brightest array.

VI.

Join in our chorus of joy, O Earth!
Thou in thy sunshine as we in our mirth,
Bright Thoughts and Fancies troop on us in throngs,
Raptures of Spirit burst forth into songs;
    All the glow of Love revealing,
      Rising with its genial power
    Through the darker moods of feeling
      Into Joy's triumphant hour.

VII.

    Aid us Music!
Words cannot utter what souls can feel—
    Mighty Music!
Thought cannot shape what thy tones may reveal.

VIII.

In the splendour of light and loveliness glowing before us,
A glory of Infinite Tenderness seems to bend o'er us,
    And blissful greetings fall
As if Heav'n would take from the earth all its sadness,
And fill every soul with only this one song of gladness—
    Love reigneth over all.

IN MEMORIAM.

[A Funeral Anthem sung by the Metropolitan Liedertafel over the grave of their President, the late H. M. C. Gemmell, Melbourne, 1880.]

Lo! from the garden of the Lord uprooted,
    A noble tree! But yesterday our eyes
Beheld it waving, fair, and richly fruited,
    Now, levelled in the dust of death it lies.
Thus sees the fleshly eye! The spirit, rather
    Looking behind the forms of things would see,
Now resting in the bosom of the Father,
    A brother's soul from prisoning flesh set free.

Dear to us was the friend who has departed,—
    Goodly the fruit his strong ripe manhood bore.
Farewell awhile, thou noble and true-hearted!
    Our hearts go with thee to that farther shore.
And in our memory more closely folding
    The deep imprint made by thy truth and worth,
Our spirits still with thine communion holding,
    We will enshrine thee in our life on earth.

THE ANGELS' PRAYER.

Was it only Fancy, playing
   With a pleasure too divine?
Heard I not the angels, praying
   Over their belov'd and mine?

Guardian angels—from the portal
   Of a loving mother's eye
Watching over children,—mortal,
   Who might yet with angels vie?

Yes! My grosser senses clearing
   Came to me celestial air,
Filled divinely with the hearing
   Of the guardian angels' prayer.

What the prayer was—though I heard it—
   Heard, and understood it well,
Never shall a mortal word it
   Till in heav'n he learn the spell.

But to that divine petition,
   Answer meet could not be given
Save by breaking down partition
   In their lives 'twixt earth and heaven.

And the sound of angel voices
    Comes to me more dimly now.
While that host in heav'n rejoices
    We, bereaved, on earth must bow.

But where fullest joy is chanted
    Place for us shall yet be given,
Where the angels' prayer was granted,
    Where our children are, in heaven.

VICTORIAN JUBILEE ODE.

Music by ALFRED PLUMPTON.

[This Ode was performed, by authority and in presence of the Government of Victoria, by the leading Musical Societies of Melbourne, as part of the State programme arranged for the celebration of the Queen's Jubilee. The enthusiastic reception accorded to it by an immense audience, bore testimony to the deeply-rooted love and loyalty of the people of Australia to the Queen and Commonwealth of the land still universally known among them by the dear name of "HOME."]

ARGUMENT.

THE Ode is composed for music in dramatic form, as follows :—The opening chorus represents Victoria, Queen of Great Britain and Ireland, and Empress of India, enthroned on the fiftieth anniversary of her accession. Songs of Jubilee arise from the peoples of her realms in all quarters of the globe; the voice of her young daughter and namesake is heard, in a solo sung by Victoria, followed by a concerted piece, associating all the colonies of Australia in united harmony.

In the following numbers the Colonies are joined by all British subjects and English-speaking peoples, owning their kindred with pride and love, and praying for cessation of all internal strife and wrong, that the whole realm may be confederate, with the exalted aim of extending the reign of liberty, righteousness, peace, purity, and love.

In the concluding numbers the other nations of the earth catch the echoes of the strain, and all unite in prophetic hope and prayer for the final attainment of the far distant day, when shall be accomplished, in the coming Jubilee of Jubilees, the grand federation of humanity, when peace and good-will shall cover the earth, and the nations shall learn war no more.

I.

Hark to the rolling tide
   Of myriad Jubilees,
In swelling harmonies spread far and wide
   Like earth surrounding seas.
     From frozen pole to torrid zone,
     Hymns are ascending to thy throne,
Remotest East to the Far West replies,
Lifting thy glorious name unto the skies
              —Victoria!

II.

Thy reign, like a fair morning star begun,
   Growing still fairer, clearer, and more bright;
Now o'er the western wave, a glorious sun,
   Full orbed in splendour, floods the world with light.

    O Queen! whose sovereign might
    Stands ever for the right,
       And rules the free;
    From this triumphant hour
    May God uphold thy power,
    Till Heaven be thy dower.
       All hail to thee!

III.

Southward, O Queen! now turn thy face,
List to a daughter of thy race;
A babe among the nations: Yet to Fame
Not all unknown. She bears thine own great name.

Victoria—
   Queen of my mother land, to thee
     This day with fervent heart I raise
     My brightest torch of love and praise.
Mother of nations, as thy children throng
Around thee, each with song succeeding song,
   Oh, warm and welcome may my tribute be.

Thou gavest me a royal gift—thy name!
A sacred pledge and heritage of fame,
And I upon my brow with pride will wear it,
And in my heart of hearts with love will bear it.

 Around thee a halo of glory
  Is shed from a mighty past,
 And the dawning rays of a future
  Still brighter are round thee cast.
 Thou art shrined in a glow of splendour—
  A glory of world-wide love—
 That encircles thy throne, and uplifts it
  All earthly thrones above.

 Awake, my Austral Sisters,
  Let selfish strife be done,
 The glory of our future
  By union must be won.

IV.

The call is heard. The Southern brood
Of giants rise in joyous mood,
Each like an infant Hercules
 But now in cradle sleeping,
Awakes in deadly grip to seize
 Serpents of discord creeping.
Th' envenomed reptiles writhe in vain
In each sinewy grasp—They are slain! They are
 slain!

In sure accord the song shall be
Of the Sisters that dwell in the Austral sea;
Across their borders hand seeks hand,
They are one in their love of the Fatherland!
In soul and kindred one are they,
One name inspires each heart and voice to-day
—Victoria!

v.

New South Wales—
    I am the eldest born, but none
        Of first or last shall speak to-day—
    Greater or less, we come as one
        The tribute of our love to pay.

The Colonies United—
    Not for the majesty alone
    That came to thee with crown and throne,
    But for the pure unsullied fame
    Of thine own life we bless thy name.

    The Southern isles fair greetings send,
    Fervent as skies that o'er them bend,
    In loving loyalty addressed
    To the dear islands of the West.

    Belovèd Queen! thy people's joy is thine,
    Therefore we pray—may gifts divine,
    Heaven's bounties in full garnered store,
    Be thine and theirs for evermore.

Thus over all the world thy peoples raise
Their songs: the Heav'ns are filled with prayer and praise.

All English-speaking People—
   O Sovereign of a favoured race,
   With proudly swelling hearts we trace
   The annals of the former days,
   Where deeds of our forefathers blaze.
   Up steep and thorny paths with bleeding feet
   They pressed, whilst blinding storms and tempest beat.
      Dauntless, their hero fights they fought;
      As saints and holy martyrs wrought,
   For God and for their country liv'd and died,
   And God rewarded them with Empire wide,
      Conquests of sword, and tongue, and pen,
      O'er Nature's wilds, o'er savage men;
      In arts and science conquerors they—
      And all they won is ours to-day,
   That we to loftier heights may press
   The sov'reign rule of peace and righteousness.

   Their glory on thy regal brow
      Undimmed, unstained, hath ever been,
   Therefore our hearts to thee we bow,
      We love our Nation in our Queen.
   God keep thee still in that high place
      Of world-wide Empire! 'Neath thy sway

May Britain still th' ethereal grace
   Of Heaven-born liberty display.
In every heart, O love divine,
   Through all the realms bid discord cease,
And govern all with power benign
   Of justice, purity, and peace.

VII.

As a mandate from on high
   The Nations hear, and echo back the cry.

All Nations—

   Thrust back the half-drawn sword !
   Henceforth be war abhorr'd !
   Stifle the cannon's roar !
   Sow blood, reap tears, no more !

   Ye winds of God, song laden as ye fly
   Over all lands and seas—
   Proclaim the Jubilee of Jubilees !

     O Lord our God arise !
     Confound all enmities !
       And make them fall.
     Peace and good-will draw nigh !
     Fell strife and discord die !
     Oh, hear Thy children cry—
       God save us all !

THE HIGHER LIFE.

THE TWO POOLS.

Upon a low dead level lay the first,
    Near neighbour to a ditch,
        From which,
When the full stream over its confines burst,
    By many a well-worn channel led
The foul ditch water made the pool its bed.

Created by its vapour's poison breath
      Foul things into it crept
          And slept
After a loathsome life in loathsome death.
    In summer, drying up it lay
A noisome thing—a blot upon the day.

The other lay upon a mountain's side,
      High up in purest air.
        And there
A thing impure might come, but not abide.
    As scum upon the surface cast
Away in constant overflow it past.

Place there doth every tender beauty find,
    By which a holy thought
        Is brought
Into the pure and upward-looking mind :
    And the prismatic hues of heaven
In summer to its last clear drops are given.

THE TWO LIVES.

One, ever grovelling in low desires,
    Foul thoughts are welcomed in,
        And sin
Riots unchecked till lusty youth expires ;
    And age, as wasting passions cool,
Is like the drying of the ditch-fed pool.

The other, in a higher atmosphere,
    Lives near to God.   In constant strife,
        This life
Labours to keep heart pure, and conscience clear
    And to its last few days are given
Light from the opening entrance gate of heaven.

THE DREAM OF OLAF.

King Olaf fell a-dreaming,
   Whilst the wars still pressed him sore,
Of a light from heaven beaming,
   And of peace for evermore.
So he set his limbs from his armour free,
   Went forth in his ship with a white-robed band,
And sailing over the summer sea
   He gazed on the cliffs of the bold North Land.

Oh, sweetly the sunlight gilded the face
   Of the rugged shore; and the tender green
So mantled its furrows that not a trace
   Of the awful might of their frown could be seen.
Their beauty, like balm, sank deep in his breast,
And he lay, like a child in a heaven of rest.

Soon from his blissful dream he woke.
   Before him stands grim-visaged Thor.
" O sluggard— with many a grievous stroke
   Of my hammer, and blastings of fiery war,
These low dead shores were upward driven
Ere beauty in fiery birth was given.

The Dream of Olaf.

"Who putteth off his armour, before the fight is done,
Or seeks Life's night of rest before the race of Life be run,
No heav'n of rest, but hell of sloth, and shame the slave hath won.

"Go back to the fight. Let valour and worth
    Be proved in the fiery furnace of war
Till none but heroes shall live on the earth
    Or feast in Valhalla with Odin and Thor."

TRANSLATIONS.

IPHIGENIA IN TAURIS.

A TRANSLATION FROM THE GERMAN OF GOETHE.

INTRODUCTION.

THERE has been much controversy as to Goethe's main idea and intention in this drama. It has been asked, "What 'moral' did he intend to convey? Why did he select a classical subject for dramatization? Is 'Iphigenia' a modern specimen of Greek tragedy, or is it a purely modern drama?"

The best answer to such questions is to be found in Goethe's own words (quoted by Pfleiderer) on this subject. They are as follows:

"What is 'Iphigenia' but an incarnation of that Christianity of disposition to which Jesus pointed when He said 'Blessed are the pure in heart, for they shall see God'? She is the pure and lofty soul who, by the divine power of truth and goodness, softens the rough manners of the barbarians, heals and reconciles the sin and curse laden dark and bewildered mind of her brother, softens the proud arrogance of men, and takes from their hands the arms they held uplifted, and who after all this at last fulfils the decree of the gods and reverses the old curse of her race?

"Thus Iphigenia presents to us the truly Christian idea that the pure and good man is a divine instrument from whom an atoning and healing virtue goes out to the world that is entangled in guilt and error."

Persons of the Drama.

Iphigenia, Daughter of Agamemnon, and Priestess of Diana.
Thoas, King of Tauris.
Orestes, Brother of Iphigenia.
Pylades, Friend of Orestes.
Arkas, General of the Army of King Thoas.

The scene of the Drama is laid in the Grove before Diana's Temple.

ACT I.

Argument.

The act opens with a mournful soliloquy in which Iphigenia laments her long exile in a strange land from her home and all her beloved ones there. She had been doomed to be a sacrifice on the altar of Diana, but at the moment when the priest held the uplifted knife at her breast, the goddess, herself, intervened to save her, enveloped her in a cloud and transported her to Tauris, where Thoas, the king, retained her as priestess in Diana's temple. Her truth, purity, and beauty win the love of the king, who, for her sake, and moved by her prayers, restrains the people from the terrible custom (which till then had prevailed as a sacred duty) of putting to death, as a sacrifice, on Diana's altar every stranger taken captive on the shores of Tauris. The king—although "a rough barbarian Scythian"—is a noble man, advanced in years, saddened by the loss of the last and best of his sons, slain by his side in battle. His sorrow is not only because of the desolation of his own home, but also because of the calamities which he dreads may come upon the wild people over whom he rules, if he dies leaving no heir to the throne. Iphigenia reveres and loves him, but only as a second father, besides, she is bound by sacred vows to a life of virginity. She seeks to dissuade him from his suit by telling him she is a child of the race of Tantatus—wild and savage beings, whose dreadful crimes have brought the hatred and the curse of the gods on them and on all their descendants. She relates the histories of Pelops who won Hippodamien by treachery and by the murder of her father—of his two sons Atreus and Thyest, who united with their mother in the murder of their half-brother—and of Atreus, who was induced by the arts of his brother to kill his own son, and in revenge slaughtered the two sons of Thyest, and set them in a horrible manner before their father at a banquet on his arrival at a feast of pretended reconciliation.

All this is of no avail. The king still urges his suit, and becomes embittered and angry at Iphigenia's persistent refusal, which he attributes to a feeling of scorn entertained by her as a Greek, towards him as a barbarian. He leaves her, threatening that he will no longer, on her account, withhold his people from their cherished custom of sacrificing strangers. Two captives just taken are to be sent to her to be sacrificed immediately. These captives are discovered in the following acts to be Iphigenia's long-lost brother Orestes, and his friend Pylades.

ACT I.

Scene I. *The grove surrounding Diana's temple.*

(*Enter from the temple Iphigenia alone.*)

Iphigenia—
    Beneath your leafy shadows thickly falling
    From rustling heights, O ancient holy grove,
    As in the tranquil dwelling of the gods
    I tread, still now as when at first I came,
    With shuddering awe, and here my soul can find
    No settled peace—no feeling of content!
    So many years a higher Will to which

I gave myself, preserves me here concealed,
Yet still, as at the first, I am a stranger.
For ah! the ocean parts me from my loved ones!
Long, weary days I stand upon the shore,
My soul goes out towards the Grecian land,
And nothing but the hollow roar of waves
In misty tones, brings back my sighs to me.
Woe, woe to him who, far from kindred, leads
A lonely life! A wasting grief tears from him
Each cup of happiness that nears his lips.
Still thronging down upon him crowd the thoughts
Of his forefather's halls, where first the sun
Uplifted heaven's light upon him. Where
The children of the household in their play
Faster and faster knit the tender bonds
That bound them each to each.

      What gods ordain
I may not question, yet a woman's lot
Is pitiable. At home and in the war
Man rules, and in a foreign land is wise
To aid himself. To him a crown is brought
By conquest;—he rejoices in possession;
An honourable death for him is ready.
How narrow bounden is a woman's lot!
Obedience to a husband's rough commands
Must be to her both duty and reward:
How wretched if by hostile fortune driven

To dwell with strangers in a foreign land!
Thus I am held by noble Thoas here,
Fast bound in stern and sacred servitude.
O how ashamed I stand that still I serve,
With sad reluctance, thee, my saviour goddess!
My life should be a willing offering, given
To serve thee freely.   I have ever hoped—
And still will hope—in thee, whose holy arms
Enfolded gently the rejected daughter
Of him who is the greatest of the kings.
Daughter of Jove, O hear!—When he whose soul
With anguish thou didst tear, demanding from him
His daughter for thine altar—when again
The godlike Agamemnon—who for thee
His dearest one upon the altar laid—
When, glorious from the ruined walls of Troy,
He turns once more to fatherland, and finds
His dearest treasures—wife and son and daughter—
By thee preserved,—then also, at the last,
Give me to mine again, and save me, thou
Who didst from death deliver,—O release me
From this life here which is a second death!

SCENE II. *Iphigenia. Arkas.*

Arkas—

The king hath sent me here.   He bids me offer
Fair greeting to the priestess of Diana.

This is the day when Tauris to her goddess
Gives thanks for new and wondrous victory.
I haste before to tell thee that the King
Is coming with his army near at hand.

Iphigenia—

We are prepared to greet them worthily.
Our goddess with a gracious aspect waits
For welcome offerings from Thoas' hand.

Arkas—

O that I found the aspect of the priestess—
Revered and highly honoured—even thine
O holy maiden—clearer, brightening
All signs of good to us! Still hides thy soul
Beneath a sorrow full of mystery,
Whilst we in vain have waited many years
For one confiding word out of thy heart.
Since first I knew thee in this place, my soul
Hath always shuddered to behold thee thus.
And still, as with an iron band, remains
Thy soul close forged, shut up within itself.

Iphigenia—

An exiled orphan—this becomes me well!

Arkas—

Seem'st thou an exile and an orphan here?

Iphigenia—
    Can foreign shores become a fatherland?

Arkas—
    To thee thy fatherland is now grown strange.

Iphigenia—
    Therefore my heart is wounded past all healing.
    In early youth, when scarcely yet the soul
    Had bound itself to parents and to kindred—
    The young shoots growing from the ancient stem
    In love united, striving heavenwards—
    Alas! a strange curse seized and severed me
    From my belov'd ones—tore the lovely bond
    With iron hand asunder. Then was gone
    The first best joy of youth—the prosperous growth
    Of early childhood. Saved indeed from death
    I was but as the shadow of myself,
    And life's bright joy blooms not for me again.

Arkas—
    If thou wilt thus unhappy deem thyself
    I dare to call thee an unthankful one.

Iphigenia—
    You have continual thanks.

Arkas—
                        Not rightly given!
    A kindly welcome would be answered by

A life at peace and a contented heart
Responding to the host with looks of joy.
When thou so many years ago wert placed
By deep mysterious fate within this grove
Came Thoas unto thee, as unto one
Bestowed by God. With reverent love he wooed thee.
And gracious unto thee and friendly was
This land which, till thy coming, every stranger
Except thyself alone found full of terror.
For no one save thyself e'er trod this shore
And did not fall a bleeding sacrifice
Upon Diana's holy altar steps,
According to our ancient sacred custom.

Iphigenia—

Freedom to breathe, alone, makes not a life!
What life have I? Here in this holy place
I, like a shadow round my own grave wand'ring,
Must only mourn! And shall I call this life,
A glad, self-conscious one, when every day
Is vainly spent in dreaming, till the last
Gray days prepared for ghosts on Lethe's shore
Who solemnize in self-forgetfulness
The mournful lot of souls to Hades fled?
A useless life is but an early death;
A virgin destiny alone is mine.

Arkas—

That noble pride—unsatisfied with self—

I pardon thee, so much I pity thee;
It steals away from thee the joy of life.
Thou hast done nothing here since thine arrival?
Who cheered the troubled spirit of the king?
And who, with soft persuasion held in check,
From year to year, the ancient cruel custom,
Which, but for thy compassion, doomed each stranger
To lose his life's blood at Diana's altar?
And who, from certain death, so oft hath given
The captive safe return to fatherland?
Hath not Diana—no wise wrath to see
Her altar free from bleeding sacrifice—
Thy gentle prayer in richest measure heard—
With joyous wings of victory surrounding,
And even hast'ning on before, the army?
Each one of us hath known a better lot
Since, in thy presence, he—our king—who wisely
And bravely long hath led us—now himself
Delights in gracious mildness, and hath lightened
Our duty of unquestioning obedience.
Call'st thou thy life with us a useless one—
When from thy being comes a healing balm
On thousands dropping down? Thou art become
An endless source of new and happy fortune
Unto the people here to whom a god
Hath brought thee. Thou preparest for the stranger
Health and a safe return from shores of death.

Iphigenia—
>But little—as a vanished gleam—appears
>All this to one who, looking forward, sees
>How much remaineth yet to be accomplished.

Arkas—
>Yet he is praised who boasts not of his deeds!

Iphigenia—
>We censure one who overrates his work!

Arkas—
>And also one who values not true worth!
>Believe me—as a man I pledge my word—
>The true and noble are devoted to thee;
>And when the king to-day shall speak with thee
>Grant readily what he intends to ask.

Iphigenia—
>Each faithful word of thine is anguish to me.
>Oft it perplexes me to turn aside
>His pressing suit.

Arkas—
>>Think well what thou art doing,
>And what may profit thee! Ere since the king
>Hath lost his son he trusts but few—and those
>Not now as formerly he trusted them.
>Dissatisfied he views each noble son

Who may succeed him on his throne. He dreads
A helpless lone old age. Perchance may come
Bold insurrection and untimely death.
The Scythian—specially the king—cares not
For choice of words. To do, and to command
Are all he knows. He hath not learned the art
To lead to his intention tediously.
Make thou no difficulty, holding back,
Refusing him through wilful misconception,
But go half-way to meet him pleasingly.

Iphigenia—
  Shall I, then, hasten that which threatens me?

Arkas—
  Call'st thou the wooing of the king a threat?

Iphigenia—
  'Tis the most terrible of all to me!

Arkas—
  At least give confidence for his goodwill!

Iphigenia—
  When he shall first set free my soul from fear.

Arkas—
  Why hidest thou thine ancestry from him?

Iphigenia—
　Mystery is becoming to a priestess.

Arkas—
　There should be nothing hidden from the king!
　Although he has not made direct demand,
　Yet feels he—deeply feels—in his great soul,
　This careful guarding of thyself before him.

Iphigenia—
　Is anger and vexation nourish'd 'gainst me?

Arkas—
　Almost it seems so.　He, indeed, is silent
　Respecting thee, and yet, from chance-dropp'd words
　I know how firmly the desire hath seized
　His soul to have thee for his own.　O leave
　Him not unto himself; for then, perchance,
　Ill humour in his bosom ripening,
　Will bring a terror to thee; then, too late
　Repenting, thou wilt think of my true counsel.

Iphigenia—
　How?　Dares the king conceive a thought which never
　Could find an entrance to a noble mind
　That reverences Heav'n?　Would he by force
　Ravish me from the altar as his bride?

Then shall my cry ascend to all the gods,
And first to thee, Diana, resolute goddess,
Grant thou thy sure protection to thy priestess,
And as a maid with love a maiden guard.

Arkas—
Peace! Peace! No headstrong heat of youthful blood
Impels our king to such a young man's deed
Of wild audacity. As now he feels,
I fear another hard conclusion from him,
Which he will not be held from, for the soul
Is steadfast and inflexible within him.
Therefore, I pray thee, give him confidence
And thanks—if thou no warmer gift canst render.

Iphigenia—
O tell me what is further known to thee!

Arkas—
Hear it from him! I see the king is coming;
Thine own heart calls on thee to reverence him,
And meet him with a friendly confidence.
A noble man will very far be led
By a good word out of a woman's mouth.

[*Exit Arkas.*

Iphigenia (alone)—
Indeed, I cannot see how I may follow
The counsel of this faithful man. But gladly

I follow duty, giving to the king
Good counsel for his welfare ; and I wish
That I may speak with truth words pleasing to him.

Scene III. *Iphigenia. Thoas.*

Iphigenia—
The goddess bless thee with all sovereign good—
Grant victory and glory unto thee—
And riches and the welfare of thy people !
Be every pious wish of thine fulfilled
That they o'er whom with anxious care thou rulest
Choice gifts of Fortune may with thee enjoy !

Thoas—
Content am I to be my people's glory :
My gains are for the joy of others, more
Than for my own. That man is happiest—
Be he the king, or least of all the people—
Whose joy is in the bosom of his home.
Thou didst take part with me in my deep sorrow
When from my side, my son, the last and best,
Was smitten by the weapon of the foe.
So long as vengeance raged in me, my soul
Felt not the desolation of my dwelling ;
But now that I return, with wrath appeased,—
Their kingdom overthrown, my son avenged,—
My home hath nothing left to give me joy.
The glad obedience of former days

Which, beaming forth from every eye, met mine,
Is now by care and anxious thought subdued.
Each one, with gloomy forethought of the future
Follows the childless king because he must.
Now to this temple, where so often I
Have come to pray, or praise, for victory,
I come to-day. An old desire I bear
Within my heart which is not strange to thee
Nor unexpected. I desire and hope
To lead thee to my dwelling as a bride—
A blessing to my people and myself.

Iphigenia—

Too much, O king, too much thou offerest
To one unknown! The fugitive, who sought
Nought but protection and repose which thou
Hast freely given, stands ashamed before thee.

Thoas—

No nation would have held it right and good
That thou shouldst always in the mystery
Of thy first coming closely veil thyself
From me as from the least among my people.
Our law and our necessity ordain
This shore to fright the stranger. But from thee—
Receiving from us every pious right
As welcome guest—enjoying all thy days
According to thine own desire and will—

From thee I hoped to gain that confidence
Which, for his truth, the host might well expect.

Iphigenia—

Concealing thus mine ancient name and race
Was not mistrust, O king, but diffidence
And fear. For, ah! if thou didst know
Who stands before thee, what a curse-struck head
Thou cherishest, and guardest—then, perchance,
Would horror seize on thy great soul, and thou
Instead of bidding me sit by thy side
Upon thy throne, wouldst drive me from thy kingdom—
Before the time of glad return ordained
To end my wandering—wouldst thrust me forth
To misery which everywhere awaits
With freezing hand of strange and deadly terror
The exiled fugitive from home and kindred.

Thoas—

Whatever by the counsel of the gods
For thee and for thy house may be decreed,
A blessing from above hath never failed
To be with us since thou hast dwelt among us.
Not easily couldst thou persuade me that
In shelt'ring thee, I save a guilty head.

Iphigenia—

Thy goodness—not thy guest—brought blessing to thee.

Thoas—

> Deeds on behalf of vile ones are not blessed,
> And therefore cease thy silence and refusal.
> From no unrighteous man comes this demand—
> The goddess gave thee to me; thou hast been
> As holy unto me as unto her:
> A sign from her shall be my future law.
> If clear thy homeward path is made for thee
> Then I declare thee free from all demands;
> But if the way is closed to thee for ever,
> And if thy race be exiled, or by some
> Immense misfortune, quite extinguished—then
> Thou wilt be mine, by more than by a law!
> Speak freely, and thou knowest I shall not fail.

Iphigenia—

> My tongue is loth to loosen ancient bonds,
> And free itself to utter forth at last
> A mystery long held in close concealment,
> Which, once revealed, hath left its safe abiding
> In the deep heart, and never can return.
> As the gods will, come hurt or benefit!
> Receive it—I am of the race of Tantalus.

Thoas—

> A great word spoken calmly! Namest thou
> As thy forefather one in whom the world

Of old time knew a man uplifted high
Above the earth among the gods in council—
Whom Jupiter to feast and converse brought—
Whose ripe experience, linking thought and speech,
The gods themselves delighted in, as though
An oracle had spoken?

Iphigenia—

       Even so!
But mortals should not dwell with gods as equals,
The race of man is much too weak to mount,
And safely walk, on such a giddy height.
Ignoble he was not, nor yet a traitor.
Too great to be a servant, yet no more
Than man among the mighty Thunderers;
Manlike was his offence—severe his doom!
Untruth and careless insolence o'erthrew him,
The gods, as poets tell, smote him with shame
And ignominy down to Tartarus.
Alas—their hate endures on all his race!

Thoas—

 Bears it its own, or its forefather's guilt?

Iphigenia—

 Truly the mighty heart, and Titan strength
Descended, as a sure inheritance,
To son and grandson, but about their foreheads
A brazen band was fastened by the god.

Prudence, and temperance, and patient counsel
Were hid from their averted, gloomy gaze.
Each wish became in them a raging passion
And drove them wandering in boundless fury.
Pelops, the strong-willed, well-beloved son
Of Tantalus, by treachery and murder
Won the fair Hippodamien.   Two sons
She brought to his desires—Thyest and Atreus.
With envy she beheld the father's love
Bestowed upon his first-born child, a son
Out of another bed.   She drew her sons
To union with her hate, and secretly
Moved them to slay their brother.   So began
The tragedy of crime!   The father furiously—
Deeming his wife the murderess—demanded
From her his son again and she destroyed
Herself——

Thoas—

     Why art thou silent?   Speak!
Repent, not of thy confidence!   Proceed!

Iphigenia—

  Happy is he who joys in the remembrance
Of his forefathers, making glad the ears
That listen to the story of his great ones,
And sees himself rejoicing at the end
Of that fair history.   For not at once
The demigod or monster is produced.

A wicked, or a good race from the first,
Brings at the last the horror or the joy
Into the world.
                        After their father's death
Atreus and Thyest jointly ruled the kingdom.
Not long the concord could endure. Thyest
Sinned with his brother's wife. The raging Atreus
Dethroned, and drove him forth. Maliciously
Then Thyest, long on heavy vengeance brooding,
Purloined his brother's son, and cunningly
Deceived the child, and reared him as his own.
Then, filling full his breast with rage and vengeance,
He sent him to the kingdom of his father
That he might slay him, deeming him his uncle.
His purpose was discovered, and the king
Condemned to cruel punishment and death
The messenger of murder, deeming him
His brother's son. Too late, he learns who dies
In agony before his frenzied eyes,
And now, to quench his raging thirst for vengeance,
He ponders secretly upon a deed
Unheard of. He assumed a mask
Of calm indifference and reconcilement,
Enticed his brother with his two young sons
Into his kingdom, seized the boys and slew them,
And made a dreadful banquet of their flesh
To set before their father when he first
Sat down to eat within his brother's house.

Whilst Thyest feasted on the flesh there came
A heavy trouble on him.   For his sons
He asks.   Already at the chamber door
In fancy he can hear their voices !   Then
His brother with a mocking grin brought in
The slaughtered children's heads and feet.

Thou turnest, shuddering, away, O king !
And so, upon the everlasting way,
The sun his face and chariot turned aside.
These are the ancestors thy priestess owns,
And these the unblessed deeds of her forefathers.
With heavy wings Night covers many deeds
Of minds distracted, leaving to our eyes
Only a dreadful twilight.

Thoas—
                    Let the veil
Of silence also cover it !   Enough
Of horror !   Tell me by what wonder
From this wild race thou camest ?

Iphigenia—
                        Agamemnon
Was Atreus' eldest son.   He is my father:
Yet may I dare proclaim that I in him
A pattern of a perfect man have seen
From my first years.   My mother, Clytemnestra,
Brought me to him as first born, then Electra.

Peace ruled, and to the house of Tantalus
At length the long-desired repose was given.
To fill their cup of joy was needed yet
A son; and scarcely was the wish fulfilled—
Orestes growing up beloved between
The sisters—ere new evil came prepared
Against the peace and safety of the house.
The fame has reached thee of the war wherein—
To avenge the rapine of her fairest queen—
With all the might of all her princes, Greece
Encamped about the walls of Troy. If they
The city won—attained the end of vengeance,
I have not heard. My father led the hosts
Of Greece. In Aulis vainly they awaited
A favouring wind, because Diana, angry
With their great leader, held the breezes back.
She, by her priest, demanded from my father
The sacrifice of me, his eldest daughter.
They lured me with my mother to the camp—
They tore me to the altar, and devoted
My life unto the goddess. She, appeased,
Refused to have my blood, and folded me
Within a saving cloud, which bore me here
In safety to this temple, where I first
Knew myself rescued from the threatened death.
I am that self-same Iphigenia,
Grandchild of Atreus, Agamemnon's daughter,
Sealed to the goddess, speaking now with thee.

Thoas—
    I give not to the daughter of the king
    More preference or trust than to the unknown ;
    Again, as at the first, I bid thee now
    Come follow me—part with me all I have.

Iphigenia—
    How dare I venture such a step, O King?
    Has not the goddess, who delivered me,
    Alone the right to my devoted life?
    She has prepared for me a place of safety.
    And for my father whom, perchance, she punished
    Sufficiently by semblance of my death,
    I am preserved to be the fairest joy
    Of his old age. Haply the time is near
    For my return with joy ; and if my deed
    Transgress her ordinance, she may again
    Confine me here. I have implored a sign.

Thoas—
                                The sign is given.
    It is that thou art here remaining still.
    Seek not with anxious care for these excuses !
    Vain waste are many words to give refusal,
    The hearer only hears the one word—no.

Iphigenia—
    No words are these merely to dazzle thee !
    I have my very deepest heart disclosed.

Wilt thou not say unto thyself how I
With anguish look for father, mother, sister,
And brother, in the ancient halls, where yet
In sorrow many times my name is whispered?
Think of the joy, as over one new-born,
If I return, the fairest garlands hung
As crowns and wreaths along the stately pillars!
Oh, if a ship of thine may bear me thither,
Then givest thou new life to me and all!

Thoas—

  So be it! Go! Do as thy heart desires!
  Heed not the voice of reason and good counsel!
  Be all a woman. Yield without restraint
  To that which drives hither and thitherward!
  When in a woman's heart a passion burns
  No holy bond can hold her from the traitor
  Enticing her from long-tried faithful arms.
  Fiercely, within, the heat of passion rages,
  Making persuasion vain, and silencing
  The golden tongue of true and weighty counsel.

Iphigenia—

  Remember now thy noble words, O King!
  Wilt thou thus recompense my trust in thee?
  Thou seem'dst prepared for all that I could say!

Thoas—

    But not for that which was against my hope!
    And yet, I might have feared it would be thus,
    For have I not been dealing with a woman?

Iphigenia—

    Chide not in scorn with our poor sex, O King!
    A woman's weapons are not, like your own,
    Magnificent, yet they are not ignoble.
    Herein, believe me, better than thyself
    I know, and can prepare for thy good fortune;
    Thou would'st unite in nearer bonds with one
    Unknown to thee, and look for happiness.
    Now here I thank the gods who give to me
    The steadfastness to hold myself away
    From this alliance, not approved by them.

Thoas—

    Thus speaks no god! It is thine own heart speaking!

Iphigenia—

    Through our own hearts alone the gods speak to us.

Thoas—

    And have I not the right to hearken to them?

Iphigenia—

    A storm hath overwhelmed the gentle voice.

Thoas—

  Can no one but the priestess hear it well?

Iphigenia—

  The king, above all others, should regard it.

Thoas—

  Thine holy office, and thy seat with Jove
  By birthright, brings thee nearer to the gods
  Than a mere earth-born savage?

Iphigenia—

                Now I mourn
  The confidence thou didst extort from me.

Thoas—

  I am a man; 'tis better that we end.
  Thus stands my word. Be priestess of the goddess
  As she has chosen thee! Yet pardon me,
  Diana! I have hitherto withheld
  Unrighteously, with inner self-reproach,
  The ancient sacrifice. No stranger comes
  With happy fortune to these shores. For him,
  By ancient custom, death is here assured.
  But thou hast charmed me with a friendliness
  In which, at first a daughter's love, and soon
  The gentle inclination of a bride
  I saw, with deep delight, enfolding me
  With magic bonds, till I forgot my duty.

Thou hast my soul within me lulled to slumber.
I heeded not the murmurs of my people.
And now they call more loudly down upon me
The guilt of my dear son's untimely death.
On thine account no longer I restrain
The eager multitude from sacrifice.

Iphigenia—
On mine account I never have desired it.
He misconceives the heavenly ones who deems them
Athirst for blood, ascribing unto them
The cruel lust belonging to himself.
Did not Diana, from the priest, herself
Deliver me? More welcome unto her
My service than my death!

Thoas—
     It is not seemly
For us to look upon a holy custom
With light and easy play of thought and fancy
According to our own imaginings!
Do thou thy duty. I will look to mine!
Two strangers have been found concealed within
A cave upon the shore. They bring no good
To me or mine, and they are in my hands.
With these take thou again unto the goddess
Her due and long-neglected sacrifice.
I send them here to thee. Thou knowest thy duty.
           [*Exit.*

(The two captives sent to Iphigenia to be sacrificed are Orestes her brother, and his friend Pylades. Iphigenia now hears of the murder of her father, Agamemnon, on his return from Troy, by his wife Clytemnestra and her paramour, Aegisthus. Pylades also informs her of the events which led to the coming of himself and Orestes to Tauris. Orestes, partly to avenge his father, and partly to protect his sister Electra from hard usage, slew his mother, Clytemnestra. For this deed he was pursued by the Furies as a criminal guilty of his mother's blood. To escape from them he fled, accompanied by his friend Pylades, to the oracle at Delphi, and there Apollo said to him, "Thou shalt be delivered from the Furies when thou bringest to Delphi the sister who is kept against her will at Tauris."

These words are misunderstood by Orestes and Pylades, who imagine them to refer to Diana, "the sister" of Apollo, whose image is kept and worshipped in the temple at Tauris, but "the sister" really designated is Iphigenia, who is kept against her will as a priestess in Diana's temple. Acting under this misconception they form a dangerous plot (in which they seek to persuade Iphigenia to join them) to steal the sacred image of Diana from Tauris and convey it to Delphi. Their plot is that Iphigenia shall delay the sacrifice of the two friends on the plea that one of them (Orestes) has been seized with madness, and is, therefore, for the time being, under sacred protection. She is also to declare that the image of Diana must be taken by her and her maidens, alone, to a secret place to be cleansed and consecrated in fresh running water. She is then to fly with her brother and Pylades, bearing the image of Diana to Delphi that Orestes may obtain release from the Furies in accordance with the promise of the oracle. The two friends depart to prepare the ship which lies hidden in an inlet on the shore, leaving Iphigenia to baffle the king with artful words which they have suggested to her.

Iphigenia is left suffering a severe mental struggle. The terrible danger threatening her brother and his friend tempts her to join in their plot to defraud King Thoas, and steal from him the image of the goddess, but at the last she triumphs over the evil promptings of her fear and reveals the whole plot to the king, trusting to him whom she knows to be one who conceals a noble soul under the rough exterior of a barbarian.

The sequel in the following act shows that her truth and purity, and her childlike confidence in the king's noble nature, are crowned with success where all the force and cunning of the Greeks would have failed.

The act opens with a scene between Arkas and the king, who partly suspect the plot, but are perplexed as to its details and Iphigenia's share in it.)

ACT V.

Scene I. *Thoas. Arkas.*

Arkas—
  Perplexed I stand. I know not rightly where
  To turn suspicion. Is it that the captives
  Are planning secret flight? Or is the priestess
  Plotting to aid them? Still the rumour grows
  That hidden somewhere in an inlet lies
  The ship that brought the Grecian strangers here.
  The madness of this man—the consecration
  Thus made a holy pretext for delay
  Call loudly for suspicion and precaution.

Thoas—
  Command the priestess to come hither quickly,
  Then go and swiftly, sharply, search the shore
  From farthest point up to Diana's grove,
  But spare its sacred depths. Lay careful ambush
  And seize them wheresoever you may find them.
                                [*Exit Arkas.*

Scene II.

Thoas (alone)—
  Terribly wrath is raging in my bosom,
  First against her whom I had deemed so holy,
  And then against myself, whose weak indulgence
  Prepared the way and formed the treason in her.

The race of man will rest in slavery
And learn obedience easily if robbed
Of freedom altogether. Had she fallen
Into the fierce wild hands of my forefathers,
And had the sacred Fury spared her life,
She would have thankfully received her fortune,
Glad to have saved herself alone. The blood
Of strangers she would then have freely poured
Before the altar, recognizing need
As duty. Now my goodness hath encouraged
Bold wishes in her breast. In vain I hoped
To bind her to myself, she now regards
Her own fate only. By her flattery
She won me ; now that I withstand her will
She seeks her way by cunning and deceit,
And all my benefits now seem to her
An old world story of forgotten days.

SCENE III. *Iphigenia. Thoas.*

Iphigenia—
  Thou hast demanded me ; what brings thee hither ?

Thoas—
  Thou hast delayed the sacrifice ; say wherefore ?

Iphigenia—
  I have to Arkas clearly told the reason.

Thoas—

  More fully from thyself I wish to hear.

Iphigenia—

  The goddess grants delay for further counsel.

Thoas—

  It seems convenient to thyself, this respite!

Iphigenia—

  O King, thou should'st not hither come if thou
  Hast steeled thine heart to cruel resolution!
  A king whose mind is set upon a deed
  Inhuman, finds enough of servants ready
  For pay and favour eagerly to seize
  Upon the censure of the deed. The monarch
  Behind a veiling cloud contrives the death,
  Preserving for himself unspotted fame.
  His messengers bring flaming ruin down
  Upon the victim's head. He, like a god,
  Moves tranquilly upon his lofty height—
  The unapproached—surrounded by his storms.

Thoas—

  Thy holy lips are singing a wild song.

Iphigenia—

  No priestess—Agamemnon's daughter speaks!
  The words of the unknown thou didst revere.
  Wilt thou the princess greet with rough commands?

No! I have learned from childhood to obey
My parents at the first, and then the goddess.
And in obedience my soul has found
Ever its sweetest freedom. But to submit
To harsh commands, or hard, rough speech of man,
I learned not there nor here.

Thoas—
                    It is not I—
It is our ancient law that now commands thee.

Iphigenia—
We seize with eagerness upon a law
That serves us as a weapon to our passions.
To me another and an older law—
The law declaring every stranger sacred—
Proclaims the duty of withstanding thee.

Thoas—
These captive men seem very near thy heart!
Because of them and thy deep feeling for them
Thou art forgetting the first thought of prudence—
Fear to arouse the anger of the mighty.

Iphigenia—
Whether I speak, or silent stand, thou knowest
What is, and always must be, in my heart.
Will not a bosom closed 'gainst pity open
At sight of sorrow like its own? Much more

Should I then feel. In these I see myself!
Like them I have before the altar trembled,
While, solemnly, approaching death drew near
The kneeling one. The keen uplifted knife
Already quivered at my trembling breast
Young, warm, and full of life. Deep horror seized
My inmost soul—sight failed, and—I was saved!
That which the gods grant graciously to us
Are we not bound to render back again
To the unfortunate? Thou knowest this—
Thou knowest me ; and wilt thou still compel me ?

Thoas—

   Obey the voice of duty, not thy lord.

Iphigenia—

   Cease ! cease ! Seek not excuse for violence
Rejoicing o'er the weakness of a woman.
I am as free born as a man. If here
Against thee stood a son of Agamemnon
And thou desiredst to enforce a wrong,
He would, like thee, possess a sword and arm
Strong to defend his bosom and his right.
Nought but a word have I, and it beseems
A noble man to honour woman's word.

Thoas—

   I honour it more than a brother's sword.

Iphigenia—
   The chance of war changes from side to side.
   No prudent warrior will scorn his foe.
   For Nature has not left the weak one helpless
   Against the strength of insolence and hardness;
   She gave him cunning, taught him craft. He moves
   Lightly away from blows;—delays—winds round—
   Yea, against strength, thus must the weak one practice.

Thoas—
   Precaution sets up prudence against cunning.

Iphigenia—
   A pure soul needs it not.

Thoas—
              Incautiously
   Pronounce not condemnation on thyself!

Iphigenia—
   Oh, couldst thou see how fights my soul to beat
   With resolution back an evil fate
   That threatens now to seize it! Here I stand
   Unarmed before thee. Thou hast thrust away
   The fair petition—tender olive branch
   Of peace—more powerful in a woman's hand
   Than sword or spear. What now remains to me
   For my defence? Shall I cry out to Heaven
   Praying the goddess for a miracle?
   Is there no power left within my soul?

Thoas—

   Beyond all bounds appears thy anxious care
   For these two strangers and their fate! Who are they
   For whom thy spirit stirs so mightily?

Iphigenia—

   They are—they seem—I take them to be Greeks.

Thoas—

   Of thine own land—and have renewed in thee
   Fair pictures drawn by hope of thy return?

Iphigenia (after a silent pause)—

   Has man alone the right to dare a deed
   Surpassing fame? May only he press on
   With hero breast against th' impossible?
   What call we great? What lifts the shuddering soul
   To list for ever to the oft-told tales
   Of heroes bravely daring, though the task
   Seemed hopeless and impossible. Like him [1]
   Who, in the darkness of the night, alone,
   Passed through the army of his enemy
   As, without warning, comes a raging flame
   And seizes on the sleeping and awaking—
   At last, forced backward by his foes aroused,
   On their own steeds he rode away in safety
   Laden with spoil. Shall he alone be praised?

[1] Diomedes, who captured the horses of King Rhesus before the Trojan camp. Homer's "Iliad," tenth book.

Or he [1] who, scorning a securer way,
Marched bravely through the forest mountain paths,
That he might free the land from hordes of robbers?
Is nothing then remaining to the woman?
Must she the birthright of her tenderness
Forego—be wild against the wild—and, like
The Amazon, usurp from man his right
To wield the sword, and wash away with blood
The memory of oppression? In my breast
Is struggling now a bold resolve. A just
Reproach, and heavy sorrow, if in this
I meet with ill success, I may not hope
I shall escape, but on my knees, O King,
To thee I will submit it. If thou art—
As thou art praised for being—true, now prove it.
Grant me thine aid, and glorify through me
The truth. Yea, now, O King, from me receive it.
A secret fraud hath been contrived. In vain
Thou askest for the captives: they are gone
To seek their friends, who in their ship lie waiting.
The eldest—he on whom the madness seized
But who is now recovered—is my brother
Orestes, and the other is his friend
Pylades. To this shore Apollo sent them
From Delphi with divine command to seize
The image of Diana, promising

---

[1] Theseus, who cleared the country of robbers from Troezen to Athens.

That when his sister should be brought to Delphi
Orestes should be rescued from the Furies
Haunting him guilty of his mother's blood.
Now I have placed the only two remaining
Of the great race of Tantal in thy power:
Destroy us—if thou darest!

Thoas—

      Thou believest
That I—the rough barbarian—will hear
The voice of Truth and Human Love, which Atreus
The Greek heard not?

Iphigenia—

      'Tis heard by every one
Born under heaven, in whom the life stream flows
Pure, without hindrance.—
      What dost thou determine
For me in thy deep, silent meditation?
Is it destruction? Slay me, then, at once!
Now do I feel that no deliverance
Remains! This ghastly danger I have rashly
Prepared for my beloved! Woe to me!
I shall behold them bound before mine eyes.
How shall I look upon my brother's face
And say farewell to him whom I have slain?
Never again shall his loved eyes meet mine!

Thoas—
   Thus have deceivers artfully beguiled
   One long secluded from the ways of men,
   Easily leading her at their desire,
   Throwing a veil about her head.

Iphigenia—
                                  Not so,
   O King! Not so! These men are true and honest!
   If otherwise thou find them, let them fall,
   And cast me forth. Exile me for my folly
   To some lone rocky island's dismal shore.
   But if this captive is indeed my brother—
   So loved, so longed and prayed for—set us free.
   As thou hast been a friend unto the sister,
   Be gracious to the sister and the brother.
   On him alone depends the latest hope
   Of Atreus' race. My father, by the hand
   Of his own wife was slain—she, by her son's.
   Guilt lies upon our house, let me go thither
   That I may cleanse it with pure heart and hand.
   Thy word is pledged to me, and thou wilt keep it.
   I have an oath from thee to set me free
   If e'er my homeward path should open lie.
   'Tis open now. A king gives not his promise
   Like one of meaner sort who seeks, perplexed,
   To put away petition for the moment.
   Nor does he bind his promise to a chance

Hoping it ne'er may happen. First he feels
The worth of kingship when he hastens fortune
To one who patiently has waited for it.

Thoas—

As raging fire and water meeting seek
In angry fight to overwhelm each other,
So anger fights in me against thy word.

Iphigenia—

Oh, let thy grace be like the tranquil flame
Of holy offerings of peace, surrounded
With songs of praise, and thanks, and joy.

Thoas—

      How oft
That gentle voice hath wrought a calm within me!

Iphigenia—

Oh, reach me now thy hand in sign of peace.

Thoas—

The time is brief and thy demand is great!

Iphigenia—

A good deed needeth no deliberation.

Thoas—

Much! Very much! For evil on the good
Hath followed.

Iphigenia—
          'Tis the doubt that makes the evil!
Do not deliberate! Grant as thou feelest!

Scene IV.

(Enter Orestes armed.)

Orestes *(speaking to persons behind the scene)*—
Double your strength! Hold back the multitude
Only a little moment! Give not way!
Cover the passage to the ship for me
And for my sister!

(To Iphigenia, not seeing the king)
          Come! We are betrayed!
Scarce time remains for flight! Come quickly! Haste!

(He sees the king.)

Thoas *(grasping his sword)*—
No man unpunished, in my presence stands
With naked sword.

Iphigenia —
          The dwelling of the goddess
Do not profane with fury and with murder!
Command your people to stand still. Oh, hear
The priestess! Hear the sister!

Orestes—
          Say to me,
Who threatens us?

Iphigenia—

              In him revere the king
Who hath become to me a second father!
My brother, pardon me! With childlike heart
Our fate I have confided to his keeping—
Confessed our plot, and saved my soul from treason.

Orestes—

  Will he now grant us leave to go in peace?

Iphigenia—

  Thy gleaming sword forbids a peaceful answer.

Orestes (sheathing his sword)—

  Now speak! Thou seest I hearken to thy word.

SCENE V.

(*Enter Pylades, soon after him Arkas, both with drawn swords.*)

Pylades—

  Delay not! Overmatched, our people gather
Their last remaining strength, and giving way
Are driven backwards slowly to the sea!

            (*He sees the king.*)

What conference of princes see I here?
This is the king, whose head is crown'd with reverence.

Arkas—

  Calmly—as well becometh thee, O King.—
Thou stand'st before thine enemies! Soon shall

Their insolence be punish'd. Even now
Their followers yield and fall. Their ship is ours;
A word from thee, and it shall be in flames.

Thoas—

Command my people to stand still. Let no one
Strike at the foe whilst we are speaking here.

Orestes—

Agreed, on our part! Go, true friend, and gather
The remnant of our people. Patiently
Await the end appointed by the gods.
[*Exit Pylades.*

SCENE VI. *Iphigenia. Thoas. Orestes.*

Iphigenia—

Free me from fear ere I begin to speak.
If thou, O King, wilt spurn the gentle voice
Of Right and Reason, and if thou, my brother,
Wilt not the rashness of thy youth restrain,
I dread the evil discord that must follow.

Thoas—

I hold mine anger back, as it beseems
The Elder. Answer me! Wherewith dost thou
Attest that thou art Agamemnon's son,
And brother to this maiden?

Orestes—

      See this sword
Wherewith my father smote brave men of Troy!
I took it from his murderer, and prayed
That Heaven would lend to me the courage, arm,
And fortune of the mighty king—my father—
Crowning my days with a more glorious death.
Now grant me this petition, ne'er denied
Unto a stranger, wheresoever earth
May nourish sons of heroes. Choose thou one
Among the noble warriors of thine army,
And set me here in fight against the best!

Thoas—

 Our ancient usage never yet hath granted
That privilege unto a stranger here.

Orestes—

 So may begin a new, and better custom
From thee and me. Their ruler's noble deed—
By a whole people imitated—may become
Sanctified to a law. Let me now fight,
Not only for myself and these my friends,
But, as a stranger, for all future strangers.
If I am conquered, be their sentence then
With mine pronounced; but if it be my fortune
To overcome my foe, then from this time
Let every stranger treading on this shore

Be met with kindly welcome, looks of love,
Rich help, and comfort for his homeward way

Thoas—
    I see thee not unworthy of the father
    In whose renown and glory thou rejoicest !
    Great is the multitude of noble men
    Surrounding me, but I myself will stand—
    Counting my years as not mine enemy—[1]
    And wager weapon lot in fight with thee.

Iphigenia—
    Not so ! This bloody argument, O King,
    Is not required ! Loose from the sword thine hand !
    Think upon me, and on my destiny !
    Rash battle may immortalize a man ;
    E'en tho' he fall, still lives he, praised in song.
    But of the tears—the endless, infinite woe—
    Of the surviving sad, forsaken wife,
    Posterity takes no account. The song
    Is silent of the thousand days and nights
    Wept through in secret, where the sorrowing soul
    Consumes itself in vain and anguished calling
    Upon the dear one suddenly cut off.
    Straightly a fear admonished me that fraud
    And robber's guile would never snatch me from

[1] Alluding to his advanced age in comparison with the youth of Orestes.

This place of certain safety, but would rather
Betray me into slavery!
                        Touching these men;
I have, with careful diligence, required
A strict account of every circumstance,—
Have asked for signs, and now I am assured.
See here (*taking the right hand of Orestes*) three stars
    on his right hand imprinted!
Foretelling, as the priest interpreted,
A hand ordained to work a heavy deed.
Then, as a double proof, I see this cut
Dividing here his eyebrow. When a child,
Electra, heedless as her manner was,
Held him in careless arms, from which he fell.
He struck upon a tripod. It is he!
And shall I, to rejoice my inmost soul,
Name also his resemblance to his father
As final pledge of glad assurance to me?

Thoas—

　And if thy speech uplifted every doubt
　And tamed the anger in my breast, yet still
　Must swords decide between us. Peace I see not!
　Thou knowest well these strangers came to steal
　The image of our goddess. Thinkest thou
　That I will calmly look on this? The Greeks
　Turned, ofttimes, longing eyes on far-off treasures
　Of the barbarian—the Golden Fleece,

The steeds, the lovely daughters.   Yet not always
Did force and cunning with the captured goods
In safety bring them home.

Orestes—
                    O King, that image
Shall not put strife between us! Now we know
The error which the god threw as a veil
About our heads when he dispatched us hither.
I prayed for rescue from the dreadful Furies
From whom I fled.   Apollo answered me:
" Bring thou the sister who on Tauris' shore
Abides against her will within the temple.
Then shall the curse depart from thee." That sister
We had concluded to have been Apollo's—
But it was thou, my sister. In thy presence
The strong band loosened, and the curse fell from me.
Thou, once again, art given to thine own,
Thou holy one.   Thy touch hath healed thy brother.
In thy embrace I felt the evil power
Seize on me for a last dread effort—pierce me
With all its claws—shaking my very soul
With horror.   Then it fled from me as flies
A serpent to its cavern.   Now, through thee,
The glory of the widespread light of day
Once more rejoices me.   How beautiful
Appears to me the wisdom of the goddess!
Thou guardian angel of our house—she took thee,

And brought thee hither like some holy form
Whereto a mystic oracle hath bound
Immutably the fortunes of a state—
Preserved thee here in holy peace to be
The blessing of thy brother and thy people.
When all seemed lost to us—no hope remaining
In the wide world—all was regained in thee.
Now turn thy soul to thoughts of peace, O King!
Be thou no hindrance to her. Set her free.
Do not withstand her. Let her fully bring
Cleansing and consecration to our house.
Restore me to the home thus purified,
And place the ancient crown upon my head!
Repay the blessing which she brought to thee—
Let me enjoy a brother's nearer rights!
Cunning and force, wherein a man may glory,
Must stand ashamed before the simple truth
Of this pure lofty soul. Her childlike faith,
Placed in a noble man, shall be rewarded.

Iphigenia—

Oh, think upon thy pledge. Let these true words
Out of a true mouth move thee! Look upon us!
Not often is the way made clear to thee
For such a noble deed! Oh, quickly grant
Our prayer! Refuse—thou canst not!

Thoas—

   Go!

Iphigenia—

   Not so! Not so, my King! Without a blessing—
   And in displeasure I depart not from thee!
   Banish us not! A friendly guest-right rules
   From thee to us. So are we not divided
   For ever, like the dead, from one another.
   Thou art as dear and honoured unto me
   As was my father—graven in my soul
   Shall this imprint abide for evermore.
   If ever to our home shall come to me
   The poorest, least esteemed of all thy people,
   And in my hearing speak again the language
   Which here hath grown familiar and dear,
   Or if upon the poorest traveller
   I see the fashion of your people's raiment,
   He shall be welcomed as a guest divine.
   I will, myself, prepare a couch for him—
   Invite him to a seat beside my fire—
   And we will talk of nothing, save of thee
   And of thy fortunes. May the gods bestow
   Upon thee, for thy deeds and for thy goodness,
   A well-deserved reward! Now fare thee well!
   O turn thee unto us, and give me back
   A kindly parting word! Then shall the winds

More gently swell the sails, and tears shall flow
More softly from the eyes of the departing.
Farewell! farewell! O give me thy right hand
As pledge of our old friendship!

Thoas (turning towards them)—
Fare ye well!

THE END.

THE GOD AND THE BAYADERE.

AN INDIAN LEGEND, TRANSLATED FROM THE GERMAN OF GOETHE.

This poem is founded by Goethe on the Hindu Legend of the Ten Incarnations.

In the sixth, the god meets with a woman of the city—a Bayadere, or dancing-girl—in whom he is well pleased to discover the germ, not quite destroyed, of a reverent and loving human spirit—"a soul of good in a thing evil."

From the first moment of their interview his influence begins to awaken the better nature to a fuller life within her, and at length the grossness of evil is cast out of her.

After awhile he appears to have died in her presence. Her outcries bring in the people : the corpse is borne to the funeral pyre, the priests chanting the death song. She follows and claims to be allowed to consume herself with him. The priests coldly repulse her, as unworthy, because of her life of sin.

In despair, she flings herself into the burning pyre, and the god arises from the flames bearing her heavenward in his arms.

This ending bears a resemblance, in its leading idea, to that of the classic Persian poem "Salaman and Absal." The Persian poet (Jami) himself interprets the meaning of his poem (and, we may say, the meaning of Goethe's also) thus :—

"Between the living shame
Distracted, and the love that would not die,
. . . What meant that second flight
Into . . . that pile of fire?

"That was the discipline
To which the human life itself devotes
Till all the sensual dross be scorcht away,
And, to its pure integrity returned,
The soul alone survives."

I.

Mahadeva—lord and lover
    Of the earth—descends again
For the sixth time, to discover
    In himself man's joy and pain.
Man with men, in human fashion,
    Ere he pardon or condemn,
All their life of varied passion,
    He will live as one of them.

Through all the thick crowd of the city he wanders,
The lot of the lofty and lowly he ponders
   Till stars the dark curtains of evening gem.

II.

Where the lone ways meet the city,
  Waiting stood a fair lost girl.
He beheld with tender pity
  Painted cheek and wanton curl.
Ne'er before had beamed upon her
  Love so lofty, pure, and sweet.
"Greet thee, maiden!"
            "For the honour,
Thanks! O tarry!"
                To the beat
Of the timbrels, her flying feet whirl in the dances:
Each movement is grace, as the fair form advances,
And sinks with an off'ring of flowers at his feet.

III.

Mahadeva—
  "Who art thou?"

The Girl—   "A Bayadere.
See, the home of love is near!
Beautiful stranger, enter there;
All thy wants shall be my care.
As bright as love can make them shall shine
My cottage and I to be thine! All thine!

Song shall lull thee to rest, if weary,
Mirth enliven thee, if dreary,
I'll ease thy feet of their burning smart,
Watch for, and grant ev'ry wish of thine heart!"

IV.

Mahadeva—
"Her tender fancy is quick to conceive
The pains and unrest she will joy to relieve.
Tho' deeply corrupted, she still displays
A human heart to my well-pleased gaze.
She stoops to serve me as a slave—
More glad to give, than I to crave.
As ripened fruit to bloom succeeds,
So Art in her to Nature leads.
Pure love is never far behind
Obedient Reverence in the mind.
But I, who behold from my throne on high
All height, and all depth, will searchingly try
Her spirit, with sharper and sharper strain
Of passion, and horror, and cruel pain."

V.

He bends to kiss her flushing face—
  Her Love, like Anguish, moves to tears.
Entranced, she thrills in his embrace.
  A spell is on her soul that clears

Love of all grossness. As she weeps
Over her limbs a torpor creeps,
And, sinking at his feet, she sleeps.

VI.

With the dawn, her eyes unclosing,
    Early waking from brief rest,
Finds she, on her breast reposing,
    Dead, the well-belovèd guest.
Shrieking falls she prostrate o'er him,
    But the stiffen'd limbs stir not.
To the funeral pyre they bore him;
    Raging flies she to the spot.
The songs of the priests for the dead strike her ear;
Through the multitude cleaves she her way to the bier.
" Who art thou ? " they murmur. " What driveth thee here ? "

VII.

She threw herself upon the bier,
    Her wild cries rent the air.
" Bring back my husband from the grave
    Or I will seek him there.
This form divine ! these godlike limbs !
    Must they to ashes fall ?
Alas ! for one fair day alone
    He was my own—my all ! "

Then the priests chanted:
"Death, sad and cold,
Wearily waited for, comes to the Old.
But thoughtless Youth lies on the bier,
Before a dream of Death is near."

VIII.

"Hear thy priest's judgment! This was not
Thy husband.   Quit this holy spot!
Thy wanton life, O Bayadere,
Bars thee from Duty's holy sphere.
Only the shade follows the form.   Her lord
   Only the wife may follow, entering in
   With him the peace of Death's still realms to win,
This is at once her duty and reward.
   Trumpets, your solemn strains begin!
Receive, ye gods, this beauty of a day
Which on your altar, here in flames we lay."

IX.

So the priests, the death chant singing,
   Scorned her sorrow as she wept.
Wildly then, her arms upflinging,
   In the flaming pyre she leapt.
But the godlike youth ascending
   From the altar flames in light

O'er the lov'd one gently bending,
    Heavenward bore her from their sight.
O'er the repentant sinner joy is there,
And thus in fiery arms Immortals bear
Their wandering children home, Heav'n's joy to share.

WANDERLIED.

TRANSLATED FROM THE GERMAN OF C. KUNTZ.

SWEET Maytime is coming; the fields invite to roam!
Let him who loves Sorrow, with Grief remain at home.
As the flying cloudlets around heav'n's dome are whirled,
So would my restless spirit be wafted o'er the world.

    My father! My mother!
      May God be your friend.
    Who knows in what far distance
      My wandering life may end?

    Life hath so many pathways
      My feet have never traced.
    So many sparkling goblets
      Invite my lips to taste.

    Therefore, on! Bravely, on!
      Springtime and youth are ours.
    Explore each mountain's sunny height—
      Each vale's deep bowers.

I hear the brook's sweet ripple—
　　Trees rustling soft around—
My heart is as a lark
　　Soaring heavenward with the sound.

Oh, wander, freely wander,
　　Casting off all thought of care.
God's smile is in the sunlight,
　　And His freedom in the air.

In joyous exultation
　　Lift up thy voice and heart.
How beautiful, O wide, wide world
　　How beautiful thou art.

WALDABENDSCHEIN

(FOREST EVENING GLOW.)

TRANSLATED FROM THE GERMAN.

A PINE-TREE in the forest stands
   With head in heaven soaring.
There, swaying themselves, two carolling birds
   Sweet floods of music are pouring.
I know to what vision the raptures belong
That thrill, O ye birds, through your sweet forest song;
   Each note has caught the living glow
   Of radiant, sun-lit woods below.
Ye sing from your leafy throne in the wood
The psalm of Creation—" Behold ! it is good ! "
O beautiful earth, nothing lovelier is thine
Than the woods in the red golden evening-shine.

The setting sun withdraws his light,
   Late from the tree-tops departing.
Silently falls the tranquil night,
   Its holy peace imparting.

Then homeward flies to its nest each bird,
And still in sweet dreaming the song is heard—
" O beautiful earth nothing lovelier is thine
Than the woods in the red golden evening-shine."

SUGGESTIONS, EXTRACTS, ETC.

Rutli Meadow and the Swiss Confederacy.

Lake Lucerne, besides being the most beautiful of all the Swiss and Italian lakes, has around it the magic charm of historical memories of great interest—more healthy interest, in one sense, than that which lends such a glamour to old Rome.

Rome, in her later and degenerate days (and, very much, even in her best days), was a gigantic robber—a great bandit, relying on sheer physical force, and using it to plunder the world, devoting the booty to purposes of cruel, shameless, and degrading lusts.

We may look upon many of the stupendous monuments of ruin in Rome with far less reverence than upon the lonely meadow at Rutli, and its simple monument of rough, unshapen granite, which tell that here the three representatives of the Cantons met and founded the free Swiss Confederacy, which has lasted to the present day. They swore to be "A Nation of true brothers. Never to part in danger or in death—to uphold Right—to resist tyranny and wrong." That was all their league, and this simple bond has stood the test of ages, and has kept the Swiss a free and united people, securing at the same time absolute liberty of self-government to each separate Canton.

Here is the germ of a whole world of wisdom and guidance for the Federalists of our day. Such a binding league is as possible and as desirable between England and all her Colonies as between the Swiss Cantons.

THE UNIVERSE.

The flower and fruit of the Universe—the only conceivable reason or need for the existence of the material portion of it—that which is continually winning empire over its most subtle forces is *Conscious Intelligence;* the dominating and fashioning power of it is *Spirit;* and the crowning glory of it is *Love.*

THE CONSERVATION OF ENERGY.

If it be proved (as scientific men hold that it has been) that not the smallest particle of matter, or any portion of the energy of matter can be destroyed, then quite as certainly it may be believed that the energy of Thought, and that which thinks—*i.e.*, the mind—the soul—is indestructible.

The fact of the conservation of Force in the material world is a corresponding truth to that of the immortality of the soul in the spiritual world.

BUDDHISM.

Buddhism is manifestly not the Atheism and Nihilism which some criticism represents it as being. The root idea from which its doctrines grew appears rather to be that the Eternal Spirit, working in Nature towards the perfection of Love and Purity, accomplishes this perfection only by the self-sacrifice of the individual will to the Absolute Will; the individual soul obtaining thereby, not annihilation, but eternal repose in the true ground of its existence.

This idea is familiar to Eastern thought, and is kindred

to the Christian doctrine of the surrender of self to God, and of forsaking the world of the grosser senses in the interest of spiritual deliverance from sin. This truth is occasionally expressed by imaginative and poetical writers (both Eastern and Western) in a manner which prosaic literalism might interpret as teaching the absorption and annihilation, instead of the immortality, of the soul. Such an interpretation would be false, like some views of the meaning of the doctrine of the Nirvana. The following extracts are instances of this:—

(A) *From the Persian classic poem,* "*Salaman and Absal.*"
"To thy Harim Dividuality
No entrance finds, no word of This and That.
Do thou my separate and derived self
Make one with thy Essential! Leave me room
On that Divan which leaves no room for twain."

(B) *Tennyson—*
"Dark is the world to thee; thyself art the reason why,
For is He not all but thou, that hast power to feel 'I am I.'"

(C) *Fichte—*
"So soon as man abolishes himself purely, entirely to the very root, God alone remains, and is all in all. . . . Man can do away with himself as the great negation, and then he passes into God."

(D) *Goethe—*
"Well may the separate self its life forego
In th' infinite to find itself."

(E) *The Persian Parable of Jelaluddin*—

"One knocked at the Beloved's door, and a voice from within asked, 'Who is there?' and he answered, 'It is I.' Then the voice said, 'This house will not hold Me and Thee,' and the door was not opened. Then went the Lover into the desert and fasted and prayed in solitude, and after a year he returned and knocked again at the door, and again the voice asked, 'Who is there?' and he said, 'It is Thyself,' and the door was opened unto him."

The doctrine of the immortality of the soul and of its perfect union with God is very clearly expressed in the following magnificent passage from the conclusion of the Persian classic poem, "Salaman and Absal," by Jami:—

"For what is Zurah? What but that divine
Original, of which the soul of Man
Darkly possesst, by that fierce Discipline.
At last he disengages from the Dust,
And flinging off the baser rags of Sense
And all in Intellectual Light arrayed
As Conqueror and King, he mounts the Throne,
And wears the Crown of Human Glory; whence
Throne over throne surmounting, he shall reign
One with the last and First Intelligence."

WHAT IS AGNOSTICISM?

If it consists merely in the acknowledgment that the circle of our knowledge cannot encompass all things, and never will be able to do so, then the Agnostic is a very sensible person, and all reasonable beings must agree with him. But the evil of Agnosticism lies in attempting to set an arbitrary boundary line between the known and the Unknown, and in abandoning in carelessness or despair the highest and most vitally important regions of intelligence, becoming thus a passive, if not an active associate with Materialism and Atheism.

It is evident from the tone and tendency of thought expressed by many Agnostics that their attitude of mind is one which would parody Hamlet's words—

"There are more things in Heaven and Earth, Horatio,
Than are dreamt of in your Philosophy."

Something in the following fashion :
"There is nothing existing, or if existing, worth seeking for or caring about in heaven or earth, excepting such as can be brought within the terms of our philosophy and be described within the boundaries of our precise knowledge and understanding."

The Unknowable.

Agnostics and Materialists sometimes declare against taking interest in spiritual concerns, or entertaining belief in them, because they allege such things to be unknowable in their very nature as far as our present faculties are concerned. But what do they mean by "Unknowable"?

Their allegation is only true in the sense in which all ultimate realities — Electricity, and even Matter — in themselves, apart from their manifestations of phenomena and effect, are as "unknowable" as God and Spirit are. And yet a knowledge that such things really exist is a very practical certainty, and a faith in it is the necessary basis for practical effort for the advancement of the interests of mankind.

Science unites with religious faith to rebuke the indifference and idleness of the Agnostic's position.

Utilitarianism and Materialism.

These are the arch enemies of the principles of Christianity. The two great camps of Evil and Good into which mankind is divided are, on the one side, Materialism and Utilitarianism, and, on the other, all who oppose to these deadly principles the spiritual faith of a life in God and the Christian principle of self-sacrificing love.

Materialism in Religion

lies frequently where it is least suspected, viz., in the undue regard and too exalted estimate of the value and importance to be attributed to the ceremonies, outward observances, visible signs and forms of sacraments, ecclesiastical ordinances, traditions, and organizations.

It would be well if this were remembered as a danger to be dreaded by those who are going with the Wave of Ritualism now spreading over the churches.

Those who are opposed to the spirit of this movement should not waste their strength in opposing things innocent and comely in themselves, when not adopted as party badges. There is neither reason nor common sense in regarding beauty and order either in music, ceremonial, or church adornment, as the peculiar property of one party and necessarily, in themselves, offensive to the other.

THE POWER OF THOUGHT.

By the power of thought we are essentially related to the infinite, rather than to the finite. It is in the very nature of Thought to refuse to recognize the possibility of a final limit to Existence, as a whole, either in space or in time. A dewdrop suggests its source—the ocean—and, because "nothing can come of nothing," the ocean suggests a source greater than itself. Turning from the outward and material to the inward and spiritual, we are conscious of some faint stirrings within us of a power of reason, goodness, and love. This power in man cannot be self-derived, nor can it have obtained in him its highest development, its greatest measure, or its purest form. It must be derived from a source which, compared with all the wisdom and goodness in all human beings, must be as the ocean compared with the dewdrop. Both in the material and in the spiritual world God is revealed to the eye of faith and reason as clearly and as certainly as the sun is to the eye of the body.

"To have reason, and to know about God is one and the same thing, as it is also the same thing not to know about God and to be an animal. . . . God lives in us, and our life is hid in God."—*Jacobi.*

"The fountain of pure love is Thought. . . . To the highest flight of Thought comes the Divinity. . . . The Eternal only can be grasped by Thought."—*Fichte.*

This indwelling power of Thought—this spiritual and divine energy living and working in man—is a perpetual suggestion—one of the constant rivulets feeding the well-spring within him of the living waters of his hope of immortality.

> " Hence in a season of calm weather
> Though inland far we be,
> Our souls have sight of that immortal sea
> Which brought us hither,
> Can in a moment travel thither,
> And see the children sport upon the shore
> And hear the mighty waters rolling evermore."
> —*Wordsworth.*

The Doctrine of Necessity.

Sincere minds need never be troubled in the perplexing and endless dispute between philosophers respecting "Free Will" and "Necessity." A healthy conscience and a sane mind will always

" Know the right way by foot feel." [1]

If a man be honest with himself he will know that in his weakest moments he has possessed more of Free Will than he has faithfully exercised, and he is wilfully blind to the light within him if he blames Fatality for his sin.

[1] R. B. Browning's " The Ring and the Book."

It is not true, as Materialists and Fatalists declare, that man is ordained to be the creature of circumstance—that appetite, creating motive, is the sole origin of will, so that when man seems to control circumstances by the exercise of free will, he is really obeying impulses forced on him from the world without him. This may indeed be true of many men and of many motives, but it is not true of real manhood. Wherever there is a spark of true mind, there is a being who, to some extent at least, is not the creature, but the lord of circumstance.

Wherever there is a true man there is a total reversion of the Materialist's order of progress from appetite to motive, and we have, instead, God's order, wherein conscience enlightens will, and will governs motive and subdues appetite. Then man learns that he must

> "Awake and fly
> The reeling Faun, the sensual feast;
> Move upward, working out the beast
> And let the ape and tiger die." (*Tennyson*.)

THE GREAT CENTRE.

There was a time when man regarded the earth as a fixed centre round which the heavens revolved. Science enlarged his conception, first showing him the sun as the centre round which his own and many other worlds were moving, and then revealing the fact that the sun itself is only a relative, not an absolute centre, revolving with its wonderful system of worlds in an inconceivably mighty orbit round some star which, again, is a far greater sun than ours, and probably sustains far greater systems of worlds. The idea of a centre is a constant one, although it has been removed farther and farther away as each point reached was proved to be only relative and not absolute, and there is a constant association with it of the idea (continually being verified by observed facts) of the dependence of all surrounding things upon their centre for stability, order, light, and life. Scientific discovery, as yet, has reached no absolute centre, but neither has it reached any single body unconnected with a centre which, to it, is absolutely fixed, and on which it depends for order and stability of existence in the universe. Imagination is irrestibly directed to pierce to the very depths of the heart of the infinite universe to find there the great absolute centre—the seat of the infinite energy which is the source of the life and the order of the infinite sum of all existing things.

This central power, omnipresent and infinite in its sustaining, controlling, light and life-giving energy, suggests a very close analogy to the spiritual conception of God, immanent in His creation, in immediate contact with every particle of it, governing its motions by a mysterious power extending to the infinitely little as well as to the infinitely great, not only ensuring order in the majestic sweep of the flight of suns and worlds around their mighty orbits, but entering into and governing the principles of life and growth of the infinitesimally smallest molecules. When we reflect that dead matter could not have produced itself, and have endowed itself with these properties of life-giving and sustaining energy, the analogy ceases to be a mere analogy, and becomes a proof of the existence of God, the infinite light and lifegiver—the Author and Sustainer of the infinite sum of all existing things.

The Falls at Tivoli.

After some weeks of hot, eager, enthusiastic revelling among the ruins, antiquities, and treasures of Art in Rome, we (a party of Australian tourists) felt a desire to turn away from decayed and saddening memorials of ancient greatness to the mountains and the ever fresh, living, loveliness of Nature. Tivoli is famed for beauty. We agreed to go to Tivoli.

Some of us went, still in search of wonders, among the world-famed remains of Hadrian's Villa, and the ancient temples at Tivoli; others, for the delight of the natural beauties of the place, or, perhaps, all sought the double pleasure, and all had reason to be satisfied.

On the way we crossed the river Anio, a quiet stream flowing peacefully along the plain, giving no hint, as yet, of the charming wonders to be revealed when we saw it tearing its way through the mountains at Tivoli before reaching its quiet bed below. From the end of the tramway we went on foot up the hill, past the ruins of the temples of Vesta and the Sibyl, and were soon in the midst of magnificent scenery. The river Anio, here a powerful stream searching its way through the mountains, and taking its last great leaps into the plain, plunges over precipices, dives into caverns, splits, and winds round rocky pillars, multiplies itself into many streams, torrents, falls, and cascades, foaming into picturesque grottoes beneath huge grotesque masses of limestone rock, disappearing sometimes, then coming, with rush and roar, into sight again from several different directions. These beautiful and striking water pictures are set in scenes as picturesque as the finest of the gorges and deep gullies among the Blue Mountains in New South Wales, or the Victorian Alps in Australia. One of the falls (there are many) is 330 feet in depth. The waters come in heavy volumes, rushing furiously. Clouds of spray rise to a great height, spreading away with the wind over the landscape. The long, driving, rolling, and mounting wreaths of mist catch the sunbeams and play with the light, hanging rainbows upon the rocks, flinging gems over the trees and shrubs, spreading robes of rich soft lace, and wreathing mantles of celestial and imperial colours over the hills sides. In a deep secluded glen is a place named "The Siren's Grotto"; the river at the head of the glen has disappeared beneath the rocks, and reappears in two falls from opposite sides of the cliffs, uniting in a lower rapid foaming over a wider space of broken rocks, and plunging again out of sight into a cave. "Neptune's Grotto" is a little higher up the stream. Here the waters come thundering from under a cliff, divide around a huge pillar of rock, and then plunge with a deafening tumult on to the next series of cascades leading to the "Siren's Grotto." The ruined temples of Vesta and the Sibyl sit upon pinnacles of rocks, looking down upon the scene like ghosts of the departed greatness of old Rome. Not far away are the magnificent and world-famed ruins of Hadrian's Villa.

NOTES TO "SAVONAROLA." (*Pages* 39–42.)

1. The most celebrated and beautiful of Frà Angelico's works are the frescoes painted by him on the walls of the small cells formerly used as sleeping chambers by the monks of St. Mark, in Florence.

In each cell, on the wall by the side of the little window admitting the light, to which the eyes of the monks would naturally turn on first awaking, Frà Angelico painted a beautiful picture of some touching incident in the life of Christ, or of early Christian history. These beautiful works were conceived and executed in the spirit and in the manner described in lines 9 to 28.

2. The weaknesses charged against Savonarola are (1) Yielding under torture so far as to bear false witness against himself. (2) Vacillating conduct with respect to a foolish proposal of one of his disciples to walk through fire with one of his opponents as a test of the truth of his teaching, and (3) Hallucination or self-deception with regard to power of foretelling future events.

3. The lady he loved was born of the noble house of Strozzi, one of the greatest of the Florentine families, but her birth was illegitimate. Savonarola was too noble to think the worse of her on that account, but he passionately despised her scorn of him when she arrogantly replied to him that it was not for one of her *noble birth* to stoop to a Savonarola.

4. When forsaking home for the work of his ministry he consoled his parents for their loss of him in the most touching and tender words : " Therefore, dearest father, instead of weeping you ought to thank the Lord that He

has given you a son worthy to be enrolled as a soldier of Jesus Christ. I study, as well as I can, to serve Him, and not allow my earthly affection to draw me from my work. . . . Then, my beloved mother, you ought not to grieve that I leave you and travel in divers cities, because all this I do for the health of many souls—preaching, exhorting, confessing, reading, and counselling, and when I wish to depart they weep, both men and women, and highly prize my words. . . . I would wish to see your faith such, that, like the holy matrons of old, you could see your sons martyred before your eyes. Mother, dearest, it is not because I do not wish to comfort you I say this, but because, if it should happen that I must die, you may be prepared."

The root and ground from which the character of Savonarola grew, may be found in the following extract from his "Treatise on the Love of Jesus Christ": "The love of Christ is that lively affection by which the believer desires that his soul become almost part of that of Christ, and that the life of the Lord should reproduce itself in him. . . . He would desire that the religion of Christ would be in him so real, that he would suffer his martyrdom, and mystically ascend the cross itself with Him. This love is omnipotent, and cannot be had without grace, because it raises the man above himself, and unites the finite creature to the infinite Creator. Man, in fact, mounts continually from humanity to Divinity, when he is animated by this love, which is the sweetest of all the affections, penetrates the soul, dominates the body, and makes the believer walk on the earth as though wrapt in the Spirit."

5. Savonarola came on foot as a pilgrim to Florence, and at the end of his journey sank exhausted in a fever which brought him very near death. Italy at that time was in a desperate condition. Tyranny, corruption, and licentiousness disgraced and defiled the princes and nobles. Among the very worst were the reigning Pope and his sons, the infamous Borgias. The poor were as corrupt as the rich, and suffered cruelly from the exactions of their rulers. They were sunk to the lowest depths of poverty and vice. Florence was then the centre of Italy, and therefore to Florence Savonarola came to do all that one man could for the salvation of the people. To accomplish this he was compelled, in his preaching, to attack vice in all classes. His deep earnestness, singleness of heart, devotion to his sacred mission, and commanding genius gave, for a time, irresistible power to his eloquence. He had wonderful success in his mission, but in the end, the severity of his truthful denunciations united all men against him as his enemies, and he fell a martyr to their hate.

6. When Savonarola first began preaching in Florence, the polished Florentines, offended at the provincialism of his language, rose and left the church during his sermon, but later on multitudes of all classes were entranced by his eloquence.

7. The spot where Savonarola was executed is marked by a statue of Neptune with a fountain at his feet.

As in a clear mirror, the power and purity of the character of Savonarola may be read plainly in his own words spoken on memorable occasions. Some of them are as follows (I take them from a book published in

Florence by C. S. Godkin. Visitors to St. Mark's would do well to take with them a copy of that little book and read it there. It is an excellent book, and can be bought in Florence for a small price): Charles the Eighth of France, in 1493, came to Florence under the guise of friendship with a great army and took possession of the city. It was feared that he meditated a permanent conquest. Savonarola was deputed to remonstrate with him, and found great difficulty in obtaining audience, but he forced his way into the presence of the king, and in the name of the King of kings commanded Charles to desist from any designs he might have against the peace of an offending city.

"Most Christian Prince," he said, "God has appointed you to a great office; but you neglect your duty, waste your time, your soldiers become disordered, and our citizens riotous by this long stay."

On the following morning the French army left Florence.

At a time of distress and famine he said to the rich clergy and nobles: "O Religiosi! will you have your rich tabernacles, your granaries, and your cellars full, while the poor die of hunger and thirst? Is this your vow of poverty? All that you have of superfluous goods, is it not robbed from Christ's poor? . . . Abandon pomp and vanity, sell your superfluous things, and give to the poor citizens. Collect alms in all the churches for the poor of the city and of the country. Spend for them, at least this one year, the money for the studies of the University of Pisa. If this is not enough, we will lay our hands on the vases of the church. Charity overrides all law."

Savonarola's deeds were equal to his words. He *did* devote the wealth of his monastery to charity, and thereby obtained ill will among his brethren. Called to the Councils of the State he became practically the chief ruler. Still he lived in his cell a self-denying life, and gave this counsel to his fellow rulers: "Purify your souls, forget private interests, think of the common good, forgive your enemies, and thus, my people, you will commence not only the reform of Florence, but of all Italy, and you will spread your wings throughout the world, and bring reform to all the peoples. . . . Your reform must commence with spiritual things, which stand above material things and make the rule of life."

At one time, when the Florentines themselves were much distressed with poverty, some starving peasants, driven by war and famine from other places, presented themselves at the gates; they were being refused admittance, until Savonarola said, "I desire much that provision be made for these poor people. Do you wish to erect a beautiful temple inhabited by the Deity? Congregate the poor, supply their wants, be pitiful to them. . . . Citizens, I say, call an auction, and sell the precious things of the church. I will be the first to put the crosses and chalices of my monastery under the hammer."

Very touching are some of his last words, when broken down by the torture, and very near death, he bewails his inconstancy and weakness in yielding, under the agony of his torment, to make the false confession which his enemies forced from him. Let it be remembered that it was only against *himself* that he spoke falsely. Nothing could be drawn from him against the friends who were under trial with him. As in the case of Archbishop Cranmer, the human weakness he displayed under dread of the physical suffering of his martyrdom, brings him nearer to us and makes us love him the more. His deep penitence is caused by his temporary departure from truth. A part of his last prayer is as follows :

"Be pitiful to me, O Lord, not according to the mercy of man, which is small, but according to Thine own, which is great. . . . According to the multitude of Thy mercies cancel my iniquities and cleanse my heart, so that it may be purged from every impurity. Let it become as a white sheet on which the finger of the Lord may write the law of His charity, in which no sin may ever more dwell. I come to Thee, O Lord, not as the Pharisee, but as the Publican, because I know my iniquity. I come to Thee, O Lord, weighted with sin, and I wear myself day and night with the moaning of my heart."

www.ingramcontent.com/pod-product-compliance
Lightning Source LLC
Chambersburg PA
CBHW031501160426
43195CB00010BB/1056